GOVERNING IN EUROPE:
EFF[ECTIVE AND DEMOCRA]TIC?

Governing in Europe: Effective and Democratic?

FRITZ W. SCHARPF

OXFORD
UNIVERSITY PRESS

Oxford University Press, Great Clarendon Street, Oxford OX2 6DP

Oxford New York

Athens Auckland Bangkok Bogotá Buenos Aires Calcutta
Cape Town Chennai Dar es Salaam Delhi Florence Hong Kong Istanbul
Karachi Kuala Lumpur Madrid Melbourne Mexico City Mumbai
Nairobi Paris São Paulo Singapore Taipei Tokyo Toronto Warsaw
and associated companies in Berlin Ibadan

Oxford is a registered trade mark of Oxford University Press

Published in the United States
by Oxford University Press Inc., New York

British Library Cataloguing in Publication Data
Data available

Library of Congress Cataloging in Publication Data
Scharpf, Fritz Wilhelm.
Governing in Europe: effective and democratic? / Fritz, Scharpf.
Includes bibliographical references and index.

1. Democracy—Europe, Western. 2. Legitimacy of governments—Europe, Western.
3. Europe—Economic integration. 4. European federation. 5. International economic
integration. 6. Welfare state. I. Title.
JN94.A9 S33 1999 320.94'09'049—ddc21 98-40777
ISBN 0-19-829545-6
ISBN 0-19-829546-4 (pbk.)

1 3 5 7 9 10 8 6 4 2

Typeset in 10/13 pt Ehrhardt
by Best-set Typesetter Ltd., Hong Kong
Printed in Great Britain
on acid-free paper by
Biddles Ltd.,
Guildford and King's Lynn

ACKNOWLEDGEMENTS

Many of the analyses in this book were originally developed in seminar discussions at the Robert Schuman Center of the European University Institute in Florence, and some of them have found their way into discussion papers of the Schuman Center. But they would not have come together in a book without the gentle but persistent prodding from Yves Mény, whose directorial skill in transforming 'cheap talk' about an attractive suggestion into an extensive commitment on one's time budget I can only admire and envy. My second debt of gratitude is owed to students at EUI Florence and at the University of Konstanz with whom I have explored these ideas. Finally, I have again reason to thank Oliver Treib for competent research assistance.

F.W.S.

Cologne
February 1998

CONTENTS

LIST OF FIGURES

Introduction

In Western Europe, the collapse of communism was taken to confirm two fundamental convictions. The first postulates that political systems which, lacking legitimacy, must rely mainly on fear to compel compliance are not only hostile to human freedom and dignity, but are also functionally incompatible with economic efficiency and dynamic sociotechnical development. The second holds that, under modern conditions, the legitimacy of political systems has come to depend entirely on the belief in, and the practice of, democratic self-determination which must assure that government of the people must also be government by the people and for the people.

As it turned out, however, the external confirmation of basic convictions has not strengthened internal legitimacy beliefs in Western political systems themselves. In the few years since the Berlin Wall came down in 1989, the triumph of democracy has given way to a deep political malaise almost everywhere in the West. The sense that the collective fate of nations is in trustworthy and competent hands, and that civic obligations are to be accepted as a matter of course, has given way to widespread dissatisfaction with, and distrust of, democratically elected governments, and to a growing cynicism regarding the avoidance of taxes, military service, and other civic duties (Putnam 1996). Some suspect that the weakening of legitimacy beliefs might be related to specific deficiencies of political institutions (Colomer 1996). This is often plausible, but it is also true that two or three decades ago there was generally much more trust in government and more satisfaction with the efficacy of the democratic process than there

[1]

is now. Moreover, given the wide diversity of political institutions in the West, it is also difficult to imagine that specific institutional deficiencies *at the national level* could fully explain the wide diffusion of the malaise of democratic politics. In the present book, I will instead explore the hypothesis that the weakening of political legitimacy in Western Europe is a consequence of the loss of problem-solving capacities of political systems which has been brought about by the dual and interrelated processes of economic globalization and European integration.

In developing this argument, I begin with an analytic clarification that distinguishes among two dimensions of democratic self-determination, input-oriented authenticity (*government by the people*) and output-oriented effectiveness (*government for the people*). Since the preconditions of the former are lacking at the European level, the potential range of democratically legitimate European policy choices is limited by normative constraints. This is important since, in both of its dimensions, democratic self-determination exists in a precarious symbiosis with the capitalist economy and its inherent dynamics that transcend the given boundaries of any political system. The precariousness of this relationship was less manifest during the *trente glorieuses*, when the integration of the world economy had been greatly reduced in the aftermath of the Great Depression and the Second World War, but it has reasserted itself ever more forcefully in the processes of economic globalization and European integration after the 1970s.

The second chapter focuses on 'negative integration' within the European Community and its unique effectiveness in dismantling the post-war controls of national governments over their own economic boundaries. Through the 'constitutionalization' of competition law, the European Commission and the European Court of Justice have greatly reduced the capacity of democratic politics at the national level to impose market-correcting regulations on increasingly mobile capital and economic interactions. As a result, national polities find themselves under conditions of a 'competition among regulatory systems' that may prevent all of them from maintaining market-correcting policies that were previously supported by democratic majorities. At the same time, however, policies of 'positive integration', which would reconstruct a capacity for market-correcting regulations at the European level, continue to depend on near-unanimity among national governments in the Council of Ministers, and are thus easily blocked by conflicts of interests among these governments.

In the third chapter, the occasions for such conflicts of interest are analysed more closely. It is shown that there are indeed policy areas in which the national governing capacity is not significantly reduced by economic integration and in which European public policy is able to adopt regulations that match or exceed the level of protection achieved in the most advanced member states of the Union. At the same time, however, there are policy areas that are of crucial importance for the legitimacy of democratic welfare states, in which national problem-solving capabilities are indeed severely constrained by economic integration, whereas European regulation, or even policy harmonization, seems to be systematically blocked by conflicts within the underlying constellations of national interests. It is problem-solving deficits in these policy areas that present the most serious challenge to the democratic legitimacy of the multi-level European polity.

Chapter 4 then turns to the national level where the currently most critical policy problems—high levels of long-term unemployment and the eroding revenue base of the welfare state—are generally considered a consequence of economic integration and regulatory competition. It is shown that, contrary to widespread assumptions, there is no negative causal relationship between the size of the welfare state and either overall employment or employment in those branches of the economy that are in any way exposed to international competition. Instead, countries that are suffering from low levels of employment are likely to have problems in the sheltered sector of their economies that are caused not by the size, but by the specific structures of their welfare states. To the extent that this is true, changes in national patterns of welfare spending and in financing the welfare state may be necessary and sufficient for coping with some of the most important consequences of economic integration.

Chapter 5 then argues that, at the European level, there are also unexploited opportunities for increasing the problem-solving capacity of the multi-level European polity. First, I try to show that the Amsterdam commitment to coordinated employment strategies may have greater potential than is generally assumed, especially when it is seen in conjunction with simultaneous changes in the practices of negative integration that suggest that the Commission as well as the Court is now tending toward a 'balancing' approach that does give greater weight to policy goals other than the maximization of free competition. On the other hand, the Amsterdam Summit failed to exploit the considerable potential of 'differentiated integration' that would allow member states with similar problems or similar institutional conditions to use European-level decision processes for achieving coordinated reforms. Nevertheless, 'regulations at two levels', or 'regulations on a sliding scale', may be the only practical way to maintain the momentum of positive integration, especially in light of the dramatically increasing divergence of problems and interests among member states that is to be expected after the eastern enlargement.

The concluding chapter then returns to the issue of democratic legitimacy. Even though European institutions in their present shape are able to convey output-oriented legitimacy, the policies that can in fact be adopted under these conditions are limited in their problem-solving capacity. However, these European policies do contribute to a 'democratic deficit' at the national level as governments find themselves increasingly constrained by the legal rules of negative integration and by the economic competition among national systems of regulation. It seems worth exploring, therefore, whether this regulatory competition could itself be regulated by the evolution of a European 'law of unfair regulatory competition'.

CHAPTER 1

Political Democracy in a Capitalist Economy

1.1 TWO FACES OF DEMOCRATIC SELF-DETERMINATION

In democratic theory, the exercise of governing authority is legitimized as a manifestation of collective self-determination. But, like democracy itself, self-determination is a value-laden, contested, and complex concept. Nevertheless, in the history of normative political theory it is possible to identify two distinct but complementary perspectives—one, as it were, emphasizing the first, the other one the second part of the composite term. In my own work, I have described these as 'input-oriented' and 'output-oriented' legitimizing beliefs (Scharpf 1970*a*; 1997*a*). Input-oriented democratic thought emphasizes 'government *by the people*'. Political choices are legitimate if and because they reflect the 'will of the people'—that is, if they can be derived from the authentic preferences of the members of a community. By contrast, the output perspective emphasizes 'government *for the people*'. Here, political choices are legitimate if and because they effectively promote the common welfare of the constituency in question. While both of these dimensions are generally complementary, they differ significantly in their preconditions, and in their implications for the democratic legitimacy of European governance, when each is considered by itself.[1]

---

[1] In the history of political ideas, Jean-Jacques Rousseau's *Contrat social* may be read as a specification of the logically necessary assumptions of

[6]

1.1.1 Input-Oriented Legitimization

Input-oriented arguments often rely simultaneously on the rhetoric of 'participation' and of 'consensus'. That is indeed plausible when the empirical focus is on local problems where all persons affected by a decision, or representatives closely associated with them, can be brought together in deliberations searching for 'win-win' solutions to which all can agree. The plausibility of the participatory rhetoric suffers, however, as the distance between the persons directly affected and their representatives increases; and the plausibility of the consensual rhetoric breaks down if—in the absence of win-win solutions—decisions are taken by majority. For most practical purposes, therefore, the justification of majority rule must be considered as the crucial problem of input-oriented theories of democratic legitimization.

If it is granted that 'government by the people' must refer to the individuals, rather than to an organismic collectivity, it is also obvious that the Roman maxim *volenti non fit iniuria* could not, by itself, justify majority decisions imposed on a dissenting minority. Worse yet, it can be shown analytically that the majority rule will lead to normatively indefensible policy outcomes if it is used to aggregate the purely self-interested preferences of individuals (Scharpf 1997*a*). On the standard premisses of normative individualism, that is to say, plausible legitimacy arguments cannot be based on purely input-oriented (or 'populist'—Riker 1982) notions of democracy.

In light of the danger that self-interested, or hostile, majorities could destroy the minority, plausible concepts of input-oriented democratic legitimacy are logically required to

input-oriented legitimacy, whereas the *Federalist Papers* elaborate the institutional preconditions of output-oriented legitimacy.

stipulate specific preferences that make it possible to think that 'the people will do no wrong'. That is to say, the welfare of all must be an argument in the preference function of each—or, as Claus Offe (1998) has put it recently: my duty to accept the sacrifices imposed in the name of the collectivity rests on my trust in the benevolence of my fellow citizens. As Offe also points out, empirically that trust is most likely to arise from a belief in 'our' essential sameness, a *Gemeinsamkeitsglaube* (Max Weber) arising from pre-existing commonalities of history, language, culture, and ethnicity. When that belief in a 'thick' collective identity can be taken for granted,[2] majority rule may indeed lose its threatening character, and it can also be relied upon to legitimize meas-

---

[2] It can be shown that these assumptions are also implicit in more elaborate versions of input-oriented democratic theory. Thus, Rousseau's claim that democratic decisions are legitimized as an expression of the *volonté générale* (which would merely compel dissenters to act in accordance with their own enlightened self-interest) presupposes a collectivity of identical actors in a symmetrical Prisoner's Dilemma constellation whose common interest in the production of a collective good would be frustrated by the equally common interest in free-riding—i.e. by the *volonté de tous* (Runciman and Sen 1965). The totalitarian implications of that assumption, which rules out the possibility of legitimate conflicts of interest within the collectivity, are obvious enough (Talmon 1955). What matters here is that the logical possibility of making that assumption presupposes an extremely high level of (perceived) sameness and collective identity. The same is true of modern concepts of 'deliberative democracy' according to which legitimacy requires a discursive censoring of majoritarian preferences that will only allow 'generalizable interests' to be considered in the final decision (Habermas 1976; 1989; Dryzek 1990; Miller 1993). Once again, a prior choice must define the collectivity (my family? my firm? my labour union? my party? my country?) within which interests must be generalizable—as contrasted to a world outside toward which 'strategic' action remains necessary and proper. And the more salient the non-generalizable interests are that must be so sacrificed, the more must deliberative democracy also depend on a pre-existing 'thick' identity.

ures of interpersonal and interregional redistribution that would not otherwise be acceptable.[3]

Within established nation states, where the sociocultural preconditions of collective identity are more or less taken for granted, these considerations might seem more or less academic. For the European Union, however, they explain the concern over a 'democratic deficit' that persists, and even increases, though the competencies of the European Parliament have been significantly enlarged by the Single European Act and by the institutional changes adopted in Maastricht and Amsterdam. Given the historical, linguistic, cultural, ethnic, and institutional diversity of its member states, there is no question that the Union is very far from having achieved the 'thick' collective identity that we have come to take for granted in national democracies—and in its absence, institutional reforms will not greatly increase the input-oriented legitimacy of decisions taken by majority rule.[4]

---

[3] There is also a sense of universal human solidarity in the face of extreme misery and death. But compared to the solidaristic claims that are accepted without protest under the pressure of a 'thick' national identity, its strength seems to be weaker by an order of magnitude. At any rate, after unification was accepted as a matter of moral duty in 1990, West Germans have been willing to transfer about 6% of GDP annually to East Germany whereas their contribution to (public) assistance to Third World countries has fallen below 0.3% of GDP.

[4] The logical preconditions of majority rule also apply to direct democracy. Hence I am not persuaded that the legitimacy of European decisions could be greatly strengthened by the introduction of Europe-wide referenda (Grande 1996; Zürn 1996). Even if it were granted that, *ceteris paribus*, decisions taken by direct participation have greater legitimizing force than the decisions of representative bodies, that still begs the more fundamental question of what could legitimize majority rule as such. Thus, to paraphrase Joe Weiler's (1995) rhetorical question: if Denmark were somehow united with Germany, would the Danes have more reason to accept majority decisions going against their interests, merely because these decisions were taken by referendum rather than in the Bundestag?

The implications are quite plausibly developed in the much maligned Maastricht decision of the German constitutional court (BVerfGE 89, 155–213, 1993). The issue there was whether the statute ratifying the Treaty of European Union was in violation of the guarantee of a democratic form of government in the German constitution. Starting from the premiss that the Treaty did not, and could not, constitute a European state based on a European people ('Staatsvolk'), and arguing within a purely input-oriented frame of reference,[5] the court pointed out that democratic legitimacy does depend on processes of political influence and control deriving from 'the people' ('eine vom Volk ausgehende Legitimation und Einflußnahme') which, under the circumstances, had to be indirectly derived from the peoples and parliaments of the member states. Original European legitimization might eventually evolve as processes of European-wide political communication and opinion formation would be facilitated by European political parties, European associations, and European media. But since, for the time being, democracy existed only at the national level, European competencies had to be narrowly construed, and would continue to depend on the agreement of democratically accountable national governments in the Council of Ministers. From an input perspective, I suggest, that conclusion was and still is fully plausible.

1.1.2 Output-Oriented Legitimization

Thus the input perspective, deriving democratic legitimacy from a pre-existing collective identity, emphasizes the irre-

---

[5] Remarkably, however, the Court did resort to an explicitly output-oriented 'modification of the democratic principle' when it justified the independence of the European Central Bank by arguing that it was better able to assure monetary stability than governments that 'are dependent on the short-term support of political forces'.

mediable aspects of the European democratic deficit. By contrast, the output perspective allows for the consideration of a much wider variety of legitimizing mechanisms. By the same token, however, the legitimizing force of these mechanisms tends to be more contingent and more limited than is true of identity-based majoritarian democracy.

'Government for the people' derives legitimacy from its capacity to solve problems requiring collective solutions because they could not be solved through individual action, through market exchanges, or through voluntary cooperation in civil society. Since such problems tend to arise either from factors that affect large numbers of individuals in similar fashion, or through the interdependence of individual actions, their solution typically requires longer-term (rather than single-shot) and multi-purpose (rather than narrowly specialized) governing structures. As a practical matter, therefore, output-oriented legitimacy also presupposes the existence of an identifiable constituency. But these conditions are less demanding than the assumptions necessary to establish input-oriented legitimacy. What is required is no more than the perception of a range of *common interests* that is sufficiently broad and stable to justify institutional arrangements for collective action. Legitimacy, in other words, can also be achieved in constituencies with a 'thin' identity lacking organismic overtones. Such constituencies, moreover, need not claim the exclusive, or even the primary, loyalty of their members. In principle, at any rate, output-oriented legitimacy has no difficulty in allowing for the coexistence of multiple, nested or overlapping, collective identities defined by specific classes of problem-solving concerns, and organized according to territorial as well as functional criteria. There is, therefore, no conceptual difficulty in defining the European Union as the appropriate constituency for the collective resolution of certain classes of common problems.

So far, so good. In democratic nation states, however, input- and output-oriented legitimacy coexist side by side, reinforcing, complementing, and supplementing each other —which is why the theoretical distinction introduced here can be extracted from a close reading of normative treatises but is not usually explicated in the praxis of political discourse. For the European Union that has the unfortunate consequence that the legitimacy of its institutional practices, when discussed explicitly, is almost automatically judged, and found wanting, by reference to the conglomerate of input- and output-oriented criteria familiar from national debates. At the same time, however, the allegedly fundamental democratic deficit seems to remain a faintly academic concern while the processes of European decision-making continue as if legitimacy did not matter.

This is doubly unfortunate since it prevents a clear perception and plausible public presentation of both the basic legitimacy of European decision-making and its necessary limitations. In my view, the confusion and frustration of present debates can only be overcome if the distinction between input- and output-oriented democratic legitimacy is accepted, and if it is realized that the European polity is fundamentally different from national democracies since it can, for the time being, only aspire to the latter. In particular, it needs to be understood that output-based legitimacy, while more tolerant of weak collective identities, is at the same time institutionally more demanding and in its substantive reach more limited.

Both of these implications follow from the stipulation that output-oriented legitimacy, standing alone, is *interest based rather than identity based*. There is no reason, therefore, to 'trust in the benevolence of my fellow citizens' or to believe that 'the people will do no wrong', and there is also no reason to assume a duty to accept solidaristic sacrifices derived

[12]

from the premiss of essential sameness. Two consequences follow.

First, if there is no reason to assume solidarity among the members of the constituency, there is also no reason to favour direct over representative forms of democracy. Second, if there is no reason to assume solidarity among members, there is even less reason simply to assume that the actors in charge of making collectively binding decisions will single-mindedly and effectively pursue the public interest. Instead, output-oriented legitimacy depends on institutional norms and incentive mechanisms that must serve two potentially conflicting purposes. They should hinder the abuse of public power and they should facilitate effective problem-solving—which also implies that all interests should be considered in the definition of the public interest, and that the costs and benefits of measures serving the public interest should be allocated according to plausible norms of distributive justice.

1.1.3 Mechanisms of Output-Oriented Legitimization

Constitutional democracies differ in the emphasis they place on preventing the abuse, or facilitating the effectiveness, of public power—a balance that can be roughly equated with the number of veto positions in their *de facto* constitutions (Tsebelis 1995). That balance is achieved by combinations of institutional mechanisms that, in various ways, are thought to contribute to output-oriented legitimacy. With a view to the legitimizing problems of the European Union it seems useful to take at least a brief look at the variety of arrangements that are in fact thought to legitimize the exercise of public power and the use of public resources at the national level.

Electoral Accountability

In all constitutional democracies, the central mechanism for assuring output legitimacy is provided by free and general elections—either of legislative bodies and a chief executive, or of parliaments that will constitute and control politically accountable governments. In contrast to their function in input-oriented concepts, however, elections are here not meant to express the 'will of the people' with regard to policy choices—for which they would indeed be poorly suited under most conditions. Instead, they are important as the infrastructure of political accountability which institutionalizes and reinforces the normative orientation of office holders toward the public interest. Formal elections, however, can only achieve this effect if they are embedded in a wider context of societal and political structures and practices, including checks and balances among different branches and levels of government, enforceable guarantees of free communication and association, and the *de facto* existence of a wide range of intermediary associations, competitive political parties,[6] and inquisitive and credible media of mass communication. Where these conditions are in place, public power is exercised in the shadow of public attention and of public debates that have the potential of affecting the outcome of upcoming elections.

It is the anticipation of such debates and their potential feedback on the political fates of office holders that ultimately supports the conditions of output-oriented legitimacy (Scharpf 1997*a*). But given the instrumental nature of these mechanisms, there is no reason to rule out consideration of

---

[6] Depending on election rules, two-party or multi-party systems are likely to emerge—which will affect the probability of single-party or coalition governments, and hence the balance between prevention and effectiveness.

functional alternatives when the democratic accountability of office holders would generally lead to undesirable outcomes, or where it would be insufficiently effective because its societal and institutional preconditions are lacking.

Independent Expertise

The application of law to individual cases is almost universally removed from the direct control of democratically accountable office holders—presumably because it is unrealistic to think that electoral responses could ever provide protection against potential miscarriages of justice in myriads of complex cases affecting few individuals at a time. For protection against the potential abuse of power by independent judges, constitutional democracies have instead come to rely on elaborate rules of 'procedural due process', on appeals within the judicial system, and on the critical role of the wider legal profession.

Judicial independence is more difficult to justify when the necessary interpretation of existing law shades over into law-making, or when the legislation of democratically accountable majorities is held to violate the judicial interpretation of a constitutional norm. In these constellations, the legitimacy of judicial power must ultimately depend on the presumption that the 'political departments' of government would not respect these decisions if they did not also reflect the 'sober second thought of the community' (Bickel 1962). Similar arguments have been made to legitimize the control of monetary policy by an independent central bank (Ladeur 1992).

More generally, the widespread practice of constitutional democracies to remove certain types of policy choices from the direct control of electorally accountable office holders and to rely instead on the judgement of independent expert bodies (Majone 1993; 1996*b*) seems to be legitimized by three types of considerations. First, and foremost, the mechanisms of electoral accountability are thought to be unsuited, and may be counterproductive, for assuring public-interest oriented policy choices. Second, the policy choices involved are thought to be characterized by a high level of technical complexity and, at the same time, a broad agreement on the criteria for distinguishing desirable from undesirable outcomes. Hence 'good' decisions depend on expertise, and the experts that are empowered to make them are most effectively controlled by critique within their professional communities (Majone 1989). Finally, and most importantly, if the flow of decisions should clearly violate the intense preferences of broad majorities, electorally accountable office holders would still be able to override the expert judgement.

Corporatist and Intergovernmental Agreement

In some countries, the constitutionally guaranteed freedom of association extends explicitly to a guarantee of *Tarifautonomie*, that is to the autonomous competence of self-organized associations of capital and labour to determine, through negotiated agreement and with legal force, wages, working conditions, and hours of work—issues, that is, that are of the same macro-economic importance as are the decisions of fiscal and monetary policy (Scharpf 1991).[7] Moreover, in countries with a 'corporatist' tradition, similar negotiation systems do, or did until recently, play a large role in the setting and policing of rules in work safety, vocational education and training, or

[7] The political importance of *Tarifautonomie* was demonstrated again in Germany when, in the spring of 1996, the federal government mobilized its parliamentary majority to pass a statute reducing sick pay to 80% of the normal wage—only to see its effect neutralized by collective-bargaining agreements restoring full compensation.

[16]

road haulage, and they are importantly involved in the financing of health care and other social-policy areas organized in the form of (compulsory) social insurance corporations.

In the 1970s, corporatist 'concertation' was sometimes criticized (in input-oriented terms) as a violation of parliamentary sovereignty. In practice, however, such criticisms were treated as being beside the point. What mattered was the (output-oriented) perception that outcomes reached in negotiations among 'encompassing' organizations (Olson 1982) with partly antagonistic interests[8]—unions versus employers' associations, social insurance corporations versus the associations of doctors and hospitals, associations of shippers and of transport industries, and so on—should presumably serve the public interest as well. In the meantime, of course, this presumption has become less popular—but criticism is now driven by an (output-oriented) concern for economic efficiency, rather than by worries about input-oriented democratic legitimacy.

In federal states, many important policy issues are similarly determined by negotiated agreement between national and subnational governments, or among subnational governments. Most of these do not require ratification by the respective parliaments. But even if they need to be enacted in the form of a statute, parliaments will generally find themselves in a situation where they could reject, but rarely change, the terms of the underlying agreement. Again, there was a body of literature which interpreted such constellations as a loss of parliamentary influence, but again this input-oriented criticism was treated as being almost irrelevant: if

---

[8] The underlying constellation of interests typically resembles a Battle of the Sexes game in which parties are in conflict over their most preferred outcomes, but still prefer a compromise agreement over the outcome obtained in case of non-agreement.

democratically accountable governments within the same polity, and under the control of different political parties or coalitions, reached an agreement, there seemed to be little reason to fear that the preferences of important segments of the electorate could be violated.[9] The more important debate was therefore conducted in output-oriented terms: on the one hand, it was recognized that, given the existing division of competencies and jurisdictional boundaries, certain classes of problems could only be dealt with through intergovernmental cooperation. On the other hand, it was pointed out that, given the high transaction costs of intergovernmental negotiations, the efficiency of problem-solving through 'joint decision-making' was relatively low, and could be improved if competencies and jurisdictions were reorganized so as to allow unilateral action at one or the other level of government. This aspect of the debate is obviously relevant for the European Union as well (Scharpf 1988).

Pluralist Policy Networks

In the recent literature, the notion of policy networks—which had been introduced for descriptive and explanatory purposes (Knoke 1990; Marin and Mayntz 1991; Héritier 1993)—is increasingly being considered under normative and legitimacy aspects as well. So far, however, neither the structural preconditions nor the logic of the legitimizing argument are well defined. What most treatments seem to have in mind

---

[9] As the German experience of the *Radikalenerlaß* demonstrates, this sanguine assumption ignores the asymmetry between policy adoption and policy change when governments must act by contract. The intergovernmental agreement to exclude left-wing radicals from public service was concluded with broad public support at the height of left-wing terrorism in the early 1970s, but its practice continued long after public hysteria had given way to more liberal preferences in most, but not all, constituencies of the contractually bound governments.

is a structure which, in contrast to corporatist negotiation systems, does not restrict access to a limited number of large ('encompassing') associations. Instead, policy agendas are defined, and policy options introduced, clarified, and criticized, in open-ended and largely informal processes in which private individuals, interest groups, public-interest organizations, and governmental actors are able to make contributions to policy formation and policy implementation. The 'network' metaphor is justified by the fact that the set of participants specializing in certain policy domains is likely to remain relatively stable, and that semi-permanent patterns of mutual support or opposition are likely to emerge over time (Laumann and Knoke 1989; Kassim 1994; Knoke et al. 1996).

The transformation of that description into a legitimizing argument seems to combine normative postulates from several sources. The first is American pluralism (Truman 1951; Lindblom 1965), which had optimistically believed that all interests in society could be organized (but see Olson 1965), and that bargaining and 'partisan mutual adjustment' among organized interests would then lead to socially optimal outcomes. The more recent contribution of 'associative democracy' (Cohen and Rogers 1992; 1993) adds the requirement that all interests should have a realistic chance of getting organized and that pluralist organizations should have internally democratic structures and procedures. Finally and most ambitiously, normative versions of network theory also draw on Habermasian notions of 'deliberative democracy', requiring that democratic associations should not engage in 'position-oriented bargaining' or 'strategic interactions' with each other, but should jointly engage in public discourses to search for solutions that would realize their 'generalizable interests' (Cohen 1989; Habermas 1989; Dryzek 1990; Miller 1993; Schmalz-Bruns 1995; Joerges and Neyer 1997).

[19]

That, clearly, is a large order, and it is difficult to imagine real-world processes that would come close to meeting this combination of normative requirements—and still be able to reach effective decisions. It can be argued, however, that under modern conditions centralized-unitary as well as decentralized-fragmented decision structures have become less effective in dealing with the diversity, variability, and complexity of interests, problems, and solutions in societies that are at the same time more differentiated and more inter-dependent than ever. Hence more loosely structured, flexible, and informal networks of communication and interaction may indeed have a necessary role to play in the development of effective solutions to the characteristic policy problems of the present age (Ladeur 1997; Cohen and Sabel 1997). Moreover, it is also plausible to argue that the emergent concept of policy networks is not meant to describe institutionalized structures for decision-making but, rather, informal patterns of interaction *preceding or accompanying* formal decisions taken by parliaments under the majority rule, or by negotiated agreement among governments, or in other formally legitimized modes of interaction.[10]

When that is granted, and when it is also accepted that the relevant criteria of evaluation should be output-oriented, rather than input-oriented, then it follows that any approximation of the ideal of policy networks that are pluralistically open, supported by associational democracy, and engaged in deliberative interactions would certainly improve the substantive quality of policy choices. It would do so, at minimum, by widening the range of issues from which those that would be included in the current agenda have to be selected,

---

[10] The argument that policy networks should primarily be valued for the functions which they perform in the informal preparation of formal decisions has been developed in an unpublished paper by Arthur Benz and Gerhard Lehmbruch (1996).

by widening the range of interests and consequences to be considered, and by widening the awareness of alternative policy options that might be able to accommodate a wider variety of these interests in win-win solutions. Hence, even if ultimate policy choices should still result from the strategic, or even tactical, manœuvres of self-interested corporate actors that are formally empowered to make collectively binding decisions, their substantive quality is likely to be improved by the preparatory work conducted in policy networks.

1.1.4 The Limits of European Legitimacy

We thus have at least four different types of institutional mechanisms which, separately or jointly, can be drawn upon to support output-oriented legitimacy. At the national level, these interact with one another in complex ways. On the whole, it can be said that all varieties of effective decision-making will be strengthened in their legitimacy by their coexistence with open policy networks in which problems and potential policy choices can be explored in wide-ranging or narrowly focused deliberation. By contrast, the legitimization potential of electoral accountability is clearly reduced by the existence of judicial review and by the power of independent expert bodies and of intergovernmental or corporatist negotiation systems. Conversely, however, the perceived possibility that electorally accountable legislative majorities might, in the extreme case, override the choices of independent courts or central banks may in fact strengthen the legitimacy of their policy choices—since the lack of intervention can then be interpreted as tacit acceptance and, more importantly, since instances of major, and highly publicized policy conflict in which intervention has failed for political reasons can be, and are in fact, interpreted as manifestations of popular support for—and hence as input-oriented legitimization of—the independence of these countermajoritarian institutions.[11]

In combination, therefore, majoritarian and non-majoritarian mechanisms are generally able to create sufficiently high levels of output-oriented legitimacy to assure acceptance even for highly unpopular policy choices adopted in national political institutions. At the European level, however, the fallback position of majoritarian intervention by an electorally accountable legislature does not exist,[12] and amendments to the Treaties, requiring unanimity and ratification by all member states, are practically unavailable as instruments for correcting the policy choices by the Commission and the Court that are based on interpretations of the Treaties. As a paradoxical consequence of this greater independence, the legitimizing power of non-majoritarian mechanisms is weakened as well.

That has important implications for substantive policy. In the absence of political accountability, the legitimacy of politically salient European decisions depends on their effectiveness in achieving consensual goals—which implies that they cannot legitimately deal with highly controversial issues

[11] That certainly has been the interpretation of Franklin D. Roosevelt's failure to 'pack' the anti-New-Deal US Supreme Court in 1937, or of Theo Waigel's capitulation in the conflict with the Bundesbank over the valuation of German gold reserves in 1997.

[12] The mandate and the operating rules of the German Bundesbank or of the US Federal Reserve could be changed by ordinary legislation, and the same is true for legislative corrections of the rulings of the German Kartellamt and of the Federal Trade Commission and any other 'independent regulatory commission' in the United States. It is also true with regard to 'ordinary' judicial law-making, and even the judicial interpretation of constitutions can generally be corrected by qualified legislative majorities. In Europe, by contrast, all these interventions would require unanimous amendments to the Treaty, ratified by all member state parliaments.

or with problems requiring zero-sum redistribution (Majone 1996*a*).[13] That is not meant to say that European decisions actually taken are not accepted as legitimate—but it means that *they are legitimate only because they do in fact respect the limitations of their legitimacy base*—which implies that European public policy is, in principle, only able to deal with a narrower range of problems, and is able to employ only a narrower range of policy choices for their solution, than is generally true for national polities. More specifically: in order to be effective, European policy must either avoid opposition by remaining below the threshold of political visibility, or it must search for conflict-minimizing solutions, or it must rely on the willingness and ability of national and subnational governments to employ their own legitimacy resources for the adoption and enforcement of controversial European decisions.

Low Visibility

The need to avoid political opposition gives a comparative advantage to judicial over political modes of policy-making. If policy is formulated in individual cases that have direct effect only for the parties involved, political visibility is low and opposition is difficult to mobilize. Nevertheless, the rule of precedent will assure general application, given that national courts and national governments have been willing to accept the rules formulated by the European Court of Justice

---

[13] Writers who (for different reasons) are willing to base the legitimacy of European decisions narrowly on the authority of independent expertise, or on the self-referential authority of the legal process, are generally quite content to suggest that policy choices that cannot be so legitimized should be left to the national level where they can rely on majoritarian legitimization (Majone 1996*b*; Mestmäcker 1987; 1994). But that ignores the effective constraints on national problem-solving capabilities resulting from economic integration. These issues will be discussed in Ch. 3.

(Burley and Mattli 1993; Alter 1996).[14] That seems to be one explanation for the remarkable fact that European policy is to a much larger extent than is true nationally the product of judicial law-making (Weiler 1982). But, as I will show in the next chapter, this nearly invisible power is mainly available for extending the prohibitions of 'negative integration' against national policy measures that could constitute barriers to the free market. It is certainly not capable of providing effective solutions over the full range of policy problems that are in fact dealt with on the European agenda.

Conflict-Minimizing Policies

By contrast, 'positive integration'—that is, European measures dealing with the problems that are created by market integration—generally must be achieved through politically more visible decisions that are formally adopted by the Council of Ministers and the European Parliament. Since these decisions are easily blocked, the success of positive integration depends mainly on the ability of European policy makers to identify solutions that will not provoke massive opposition. It is this need for avoiding, or at least minimizing, conflict which explains the proliferation of 'comitology' in European policy processes (Pedler and Schaefer 1996). On the theoretical side, it may also account for the fact that, in spite of unresolved conceptual problems (Kassim 1994), the 'network' metaphor not only continues to be used for describing European processes of policy formation and implementation (Héritier 1993; Pappi and Schnorpfeil 1996), but it has also been elevated to the status of a major legitimizing argument in the normative context of discussions about the European democratic deficit (Pitschas 1994; Peterson 1995; Benz and

---

[14] The willingness seems to be more limited in the core areas of national private law (Caruso 1997).

Lehmbruch 1996; Jachtenfuchs and Kohler-Koch 1996; Ladeur 1997). Indeed, if European policy networks should be able to assure win-win solutions that satisfy all interests affected, output-oriented legitimacy would be assured, and the democratic deficit would cease to matter. As I will show below, however, the range of policy problems for which this can be expected tends to be severely limited.

Borrowed National Legitimacy

If major controversy cannot be avoided, however, the effectiveness of European policy depends entirely on the willingness and ability of national governments to confront opposition by relying on their own majoritarian legitimacy bases. It is thus not merely position-oriented institutional self-interest that compels national governments to insist on the continuing centrality of the Council of Ministers and on high consensus requirements for Council decisions (Scharpf 1988). If they must bear the political brunt, they must want to retain political control.[15] In areas where governments are in agreement, they may thus be able to override domestic opposition through joint action at the European level.[16] By the same token, however, where governments themselves pursue or defend conflicting interests, politically salient policy choices at the European level are likely to be blocked in the Council of Ministers. The policy areas where this is likely to be true will be discussed in Chapter 3 below.

[15] Since voters cannot vent their anger on 'Brussels' (and are not obliged to be 'fair') I am not much persuaded by the 'intergovernmentalist' assumption that national governments should be able to deflect domestic dissatisfaction by putting the blame on Europe (Moravcsik 1994). At any rate, the 1997 French elections did not come out that way.

[16] This possibility is emphasized by 'intergovernmentalist' interpretations of European policy processes (Garrett 1992; Moravcsik 1994).

[25]

1.1.5 Legitimacy and Capability

The implication is, therefore, that Europe will not be capable of positive action on issues where national governments, and the interests they represent, are in conflict. But what difference does it make for output-oriented democratic legitimacy if European policy should not be able to deal effectively with some classes of politically salient problems? To discuss this question, it is now necessary to return to the original distinction between the input and output dimensions of democratic self-determination.

In both dimensions, it should have become clear, legitimacy cannot be considered an all-or-nothing proposition. Input-oriented authenticity cannot mean spontaneous and unanimous approval, nor can output-oriented effectiveness be equated with omnipotence. Nevertheless, choices imposed by actors that are in no way empowered by, and accountable to, the constituency in question (say, by a military government) would lack input legitimacy, whatever their merits in the output dimension might be. Similarly, when external constraints are so tight as to leave no room for significant political choices, even formal ratification by democratically accountable representatives will not add output legitimacy to the compulsion of necessity.

The implication is, therefore, that democratic legitimacy expands if decisions that were previously compelled by external necessity, or taken by non-accountable authority, become the object of authentic and effective collective choice. Conversely, legitimacy is reduced when policy areas that were previously the object of authentic and effective political choices in democratically constituted polities are pre-empted either by newly arising necessities or by coming under the control of politically non-accountable authorities. This, I suggest, is happening world-wide in the relationship between political democracy and the capitalist economy, and it is happening with particular force in the democratic welfare states of Western Europe.

It may be an exaggeration to conclude that this implies 'The End of Democracy' (Guéhenno 1993), but the loss of authentic and effective self-determination seems significant and visible enough to explain the present sense of malaise in democratic polities. Their citizens are now confronted with the fact that the institutions of social protection and industrial citizenship, freely chosen only a few decades ago, are dismantled under the alleged compulsion of an economy that once was, but no longer seems to be, under the effective control of democratically accountable governments. At the same time, they are told that ever more important decisions that used to be taken, and on occasion reversed, by democratically elected parliamentary majorities are now coming down from authorities in Brussels that cannot be expelled in the next election. Worse yet: all of this is not just happening by objective compulsion or external force—it is happening with the complicity of democratically elected governments that must translate economic necessity into public policy, and that participate in the formation of, and must take responsibility for, the implementation of European policies. In other words, the established mechanisms of democratic self-determination are not just displaced, or reduced in their scope, but they are being corrupted and hence delegitimized by exogenous influences. Or so it seems.

The present book will not be able to cover all of that ground. But it will examine the extent to which changes in the political economy of capitalist democracies are reducing the effectiveness of democratic self-determination at the national level, and the extent to which this loss may, or may not, be compensated through gains of political control at the European level. More specifically, I will argue that the general constraints on national policy choices that have resulted from economic 'globalization' are intensified and tightened through the legal force of 'negative integration' in the European Community. While it is also true that the European Community provides opportunities for 'positive integration' that are not available at the global level, I will try to show that these options are specifically limited in those policy areas that are critical for the survival of welfare state regimes—which, in turn, have become central elements of output-oriented legitimacy at the national level. In the concluding chapters of the book, I will then discuss national and European policy options that could increase the effectiveness of political problem-solving at both levels.

1.2 THE POLITICAL ECONOMY OF CAPITALIST DEMOCRACIES

The output-oriented criterion of problem-solving effectiveness certainly cannot be equated with omnipotence. Even during the early post-war decades, when national problem-solving capabilities had reached their apex, policy choices were always constrained by internal and external factors beyond the control of democratically accountable office holders. Internally, constitutions with a bill of rights and institutional checks and balances, enforced by judicial review, are the most important legal constraints; in addition there are always resource constraints and, less obviously, there is the need to respect a good deal of autonomy of functional subsystems—like the economy, science, education, health care, or the arts—with whose internal logic and professional criteria the democratic state would, with good reason, hesitate to interfere (Willke 1983). Externally, the 'sovereignty' of the nation state is territorially limited, yet many of the problems that will be of concern to its citizens are affected by factors crossing national boundaries. For military security, that has always been obvious, but it has also become true for international terrorism and organized crime, for transnational and global environmental pollution, for transnational migration, and for global communication. All of these border-crossing effects have significantly increased by comparison to the early post-war decades, and all of these challenge the capacity of the democratic nation state autonomously to shape the collective fate of its citizens. However, the major constraint on democratic self-determination within national boundaries arises from the reintegration of global capital markets and transnational markets for goods and services.

1.2.1 Capitalist Democracy: A Precarious Symbiosis

The democratic state and the capitalist economy coexist in symbiotic interdependence. On the one hand, the productivity and profitability of advanced capitalist economies depends not only on the definition and protection of property rights and contractual obligations by the legal and police systems of the state, but also on the provision of public infrastructure, including education and basic research, and a wide variety of public services. Conversely, the political viability of the democratic state has come to depend crucially on the performance of national economies, which directly determines the incomes and employment opportunities of citizens and voters, and which generates the tax revenues to finance public services and welfare spending. At the same time, however, this symbiotic relationship is characterized by fundamental tensions: the sovereignty of the state is territorially limited, while the capitalist economy tends toward global interaction. The logic of capitalist accumulation and of market competition compels enterprises to exploit all factors of production, natural as well as human, and to externalize the social and the environmental costs of this exploitation. The capitalist economy, moreover, will not only generate material abundance for consumers, jobs for workers, and tax revenue for governments, but also highly unequal income distributions, regional and sectoral winners and losers, and cyclical and structural crises which may result in mass unemployment and mass poverty. The democratic state, by contrast, derives its claim to legitimacy from a commitment to the public interest and to distributive justice, and governments are constrained, through the mechanisms of electoral accountability, to orient their policies toward the interests of the broad majority of its voters. They are therefore under political pressure to protect groups in the electorate against the losses caused by structural change, to prevent mass unemployment, to regulate labour markets and production processes in the interest of the workers affected, and to achieve a normatively defensible distribution of incomes.

In following their own logic, therefore, democratic governments will want to inhibit the 'creative destruction' associated with dynamic capitalism, and they will tend to reduce the income differentials between winners and losers in the market. In doing so, however, they run into two basic difficulties, one informational and one structural. With regard to the former, the collapse of communist systems is also taken to have confirmed the Hayekian thesis that there is no way in which governments could efficiently coordinate the demands of tens or hundreds of millions of consumers for millions of products produced by hundreds of thousands of firms using thousands of different types of resources. Instead, the efficiency of the capitalist economy depends on the ability of profit-oriented investors and of competing firms to seek out and use local information about consumer demands and production possibilities that could never be centralized to begin with and which, if centralized, would lead to unmanageable information overload at the centre. Thus, if the state intervenes in the economy, it is likely to interfere with, and potentially to disable, the intelligence of decentralized information processing and, ultimately, to paralyse the dynamism of the capitalist economy (Hayek 1944; 1945; Streit 1993). Moreover, if state intervention is considered a political option at all, it may also be instrumentalized by well-organized and well-informed pressure groups in the economy itself for purposes that will serve the rent-seeking interests of 'distributive coalitions', rather than the public interest which, from the normative perspective of welfare economics, might perhaps justify state intervention under conditions that could be analytically characterized as market failures (Olson 1982).

The second difficulty of political intervention arises from a structural asymmetry: political interest focuses on the output side of the economic process, on products that increase general welfare, on the employment opportunities, and on the externalities associated with processes of production. The capitalist economy, however, is controlled from the side of capital inputs: capital owners must be motivated to invest in production capacities which, together with the necessary labour inputs, will ultimately result in marketable products. But whereas the investment decisions that drive the economic process are motivated by the anticipation of future profits, government intervention (and the collective-bargaining strategies of powerful unions) will generally have the effect of reducing the post-tax incomes from capital investments.

On the face of it, this may appear as a symmetric constellation of mutual dependence: capital owners must invest and create jobs in order to achieve a profit, whereas unions and governments must allow capital owners to achieve a profit in order to benefit from employment, wage income, and tax revenues. But that is a spurious symmetry. While governments and workers are indeed without alternatives, *capital owners do have a choice*. If they find it unattractive to invest in job-creating productive assets, they may instead opt for speculative or interest-bearing financial assets, they may buy gold and other value-conserving assets, or they might simply consume, rather than invest, their savings. In other words, in a capitalist economy governments and unions combined do not have the power to reduce the rate of return on productive investments below that of the next-best alternative available to capital owners,[17] and they never have the power to reduce the rate of return below zero, and still expect production and employment to continue. Moreover, since from the point of view of the investor it is the *cumulative* effect of taxes, regulations, and collective-bargaining agreements which affects profitability, all of the political actors involved—local, regional, and national governments with their functional subdivisions, and labour unions—must be extremely cautious in their dealings with the economy, lest they reduce the incentives for productive investments on which they all depend.

In the political-economy literature of the 1970s, these tensions were elevated to the status of self-destructive

---

[17] From a left-of-centre political perspective, the secular rise of government indebtedness after the mid-1970s should therefore appear as an unmitigated disaster: it has provided capital owners with perfectly secure and reasonably profitable alternatives to employment-creating real investments, and it must use general tax revenues that are increasingly collected from wage earners to pay for the debt service to capital owners. Under the lure of Keynesian economics, unfortunately, left-wing political parties and labour unions have come to ignore these redistributive consequences of deficit spending.

'contradictions' of capitalist democracies. On the left, theories of 'late capitalism' predicted an imminent and inevitable 'legitimacy crisis' of the state—which was compelled to instrumentalize its democratically based power in order to fulfil the ever more demanding functional requisites of the capitalist economy, and to respect capital interests which could not, themselves, be normatively justified under the criterion of 'generalizability' (Offe 1972; 1984; Habermas 1973; 1976). On the conservative side, by contrast, theories of 'overloaded government' predicted an inflation of political demands in competitive mass democracies which would force governments to intensify taxation and economic regulation to an extent that would eventually destroy the viability of capitalist economies (Crozier et al. 1975; Hennis et al. 1977; 1979). From either perspective, therefore, the precarious symbiosis of the democratic state and the capitalist economy could not last.

Against these predictions of inevitable collapse, it seems necessary to remind oneself of the fact that capitalist democracies have in fact worked very well during *les trente glorieuses* after the Second World War. They succeeded, by and large, in exploiting the capitalist capacity for technical progress and dynamic growth; they learned to dampen the cycles of economic booms and recessions, and to avoid mass unemployment; they were able to impose regulatory constraints on the capitalist exploitation of human and natural resources; and they developed welfare-state correctives for the injustices of capitalist distribution—and they managed to do all this without going down the Hayekian 'Road to Serfdom' (Hayek 1944). But it is even more important to realize that this 'democratic civilization' of dynamic capitalism occurred under exceptional, and perhaps historically unique, conditions regarding the relationship between the state and the economy.

[33]

1.2.2 The 'Great Transformation': A Brief Respite?

By their own logic, profit-oriented economic interactions tend to ignore national boundaries and to evolve toward global integration; by contrast, political interventions are constrained by the boundaries of the territorial state. Thus, unless the nation state is able and willing to control border-crossing transactions, the attempt to control economic processes within national boundaries can always be counteracted by external influences—capital inflows or outflows, import competition or foreign buyouts, mass immigration or tax flight and brain drain. –

The period between 1870 and the First World War was indeed characterized by open capital markets, free trade, and free migration. Under the gold standard, all currencies were convertible at fixed exchange rates, and in the absence of capital export controls, money could freely flow to the most profitable uses throughout the capitalist world. Before 1914, in fact, foreign direct investment had reached levels that were only again surpassed in the 1980s (Hirst and Thompson 1995). Similarly, under British leadership, free trade became the general rule on the markets for industrial goods; and protectionism, where it was still practised at all, was generally limited to markets for agricultural goods. In short, the capitalist world of that period (though of course much smaller than now) could indeed be described as an integrated market for capital and industrial goods—and to a lesser degree for services and labour as well. It was in fact not under the control either of national governments or of an international regulatory regime—and it was, by and large, the world which Marx and Engels had described: with rapid technological progress and great gains in material wealth, but also with great inequality, exploitation, deep cyclical crises and crashes of financial markets (Kindleberger 1978), and misery for the masses. But

since most governments were not yet democratically accountable to the masses, it also was a world without major legitimacy crises.

After the First World War, the gold standard and free
trade were re-established, but the mobilization of the masses
for the war effort had generally been accompanied not only by
the spread of universal suffrage and democratic accountability, but also by the removal of legal restrictions on trade union
activity, and by the introduction or expansion of at least some
minimal forms of social security for conditions of unemployment, disability, sickness, and old-age poverty. Thus, when
the crisis proneness of international capitalism reasserted itself with a vengeance at the end of the 1920s, the minimal
welfare state was directly involved: mass unemployment destroyed the financial viability of the new social-security systems, and the political protest of the impoverished masses not
only affected the survival of governments of the day, but it
threatened, and in the case of Weimar Germany destroyed,
the legitimacy of democratic government as such. For that
reason, governments everywhere were forced to react in one
way or another to the Great Depression. They did so by
reasserting control over their economic boundaries and, in
the process, destroying the integrated world economy.

In the early 1930s, the major industrial nations in fact
responded to the Great Depression with protectionist, or
even autarkist, strategies of competitive devaluation, rigid
controls of capital transfers, protective tariffs, quantitative
import restrictions, and subsidized exports (Kindleberger
1973; Rothermund 1993). As a result, the world economy
collapsed with disastrous consequences for output and employment. (Kindleberger 1995). Nevertheless, as a consequence of this 'Great Transformation' (Polanyi 1957), the
boundaries of the territorial state had for a time become coex-
tensive with the effective boundaries of markets for capital,

goods, services, and labour (Winkel 1985). Moreover, behind these protectionist barriers, national policy makers also learned to use the Keynesian techniques of macro-economic intervention in the capitalist economy without pre-empting micro-economic choices of producers and consumers. ➤

The boundaries of national economies were, of course, not impermeable. What mattered was that transactions across them were under the *potential* control of national governments, and that they continued to be impeded by significant tariff and non-tariff barriers and other transaction costs. As a consequence, capital owners were largely restricted to investment opportunities within the national economy, and firms were mainly confronted by domestic competitors. The relative importance of international trade increased only gradually; and since governments could control imports and exchange rates, the international competitiveness of national producers was not a major issue.

While these conditions lasted, government interest rate policy was able to define the minimal rate of return on financial investments and thus the relative attractiveness of financial and real investments. If interest rates were lowered, job-creating real investments became relatively more attractive, and vice versa. At the same time, government policy on taxation and deficit spending had a direct and undiluted impact on aggregate domestic demand. Thus, Keynesian demand management was generally able to smooth the business cycle and to maintain full employment and steady economic growth,[18] which then permitted the expansion of mass in-

---

[18] During the 'stagflation' crisis of the early and mid-1970s, it became obvious that Keynesian demand management of the Anglo-American variety was unable to deal with inflationary pressures and rising unemployment at the same time. Where stagflation was in fact overcome, success depended on neo-corporatist institutional conditions that allowed unions to assume responsibility for containing wage-push inflation while demand-side fiscal

[36]

comes, public services, and welfare transfers. Equally important: within national boundaries, government regulations and
nation-wide collective-bargaining agreements were able to
control the conditions of production without undercutting
the viability of capitalist accumulation. Since the external
boundaries could be controlled, all relevant competitors were
producing under the same regime—with the consequence
that the costs of regulation could be passed on to consumers.
Hence the rate of return on investment was not necessarily
affected by high levels of regulation and union power.[19]

During the same period, world markets for goods, services,
and capital were gradually liberalized and integrated again
within the framework of American-led international economic regimes (Keohane 1984). But these regimes were
meant to, and did, establish a form of 'embedded liberalism'
that still allowed national governments to protect the welfare
of their citizens against external disruptions (Ruggie 1982).
Within that framework, the industrial nations of Western
Europe developed distinctly national versions of the capitalist welfare state. Despite the considerable differences
between the 'Social-Democratic', 'Corporatist', or 'Liberal'
variants (Esping-Andersen 1990), however, all of them
were remarkably successful in maintaining and promoting
a vigorous capitalist economy, while also controlling, in

and monetary strategies continued to assure full employment (Scharpf
1991).

[19] In the neo-Marxist political-economy literature, much was made of
declining shares of profit in the post-war decades as an indicator of the
unresolvable contradiction between the capitalist economy and the democratic state. But since investment would cease when the rate of return on
capital became negative, governments and unions would become aware of
the risks of a profit squeeze for employment and growth—and economies
with neo-corporatist institutional structures are in theory, and were in fact,
quite capable of avoiding or correcting such strategic blunders (Wallerstein
1990).

different ways and to different degrees, the destructive tendencies of unfettered capitalism in the interest of specific social, cultural, and/or ecological values (Scharpf 1991; Merkel 1993*a*).

1.2.3 Boundary Control Lost Again

Things changed radically, however, when the breakdown of the Bretton Woods regime of fixed, but adjustable, exchange rates, combined with the oil-price crises of the 1970s, unleashed an explosive growth of 'offshore' financial markets in places that were not under the effective control of any of the major central banks (Kapstein 1994). At the same time, technological innovations and the increasing importance of multinational firms undercut the effectiveness of national controls over capital transfers (Cerny 1994). As a consequence, financial assets are now mobile around the globe, and the minimal rate of return that investors can expect is again determined by global financial markets,[20] rather than by national monetary policy. Moreover, real interest rates were generally about twice as high after the early 1980s as they used to be in the 1960s.[21] So if a government should now try to reduce interest rates below the international level, this would no longer stimulate job-creating real investment in the national economy, but would drive capital out of the country, causing

[20] The empirical evidence that capital is still not in fact perfectly mobile, and that differences in real interest rates remain, is explained by information asymmetries, rather than by state policies impeding mobility (Gordon and Bovenberg 1996).

[21] The reasons for this secular rise of real interest rates are not well understood, but it seems clear that the dramatic rise of government indebtedness after the oil-price crises of the 1970s as well as the 'monetarist' shift of central bank priorities, from assuring full employment to the fight against inflation, must be part of any explanation.

devaluation and a rising rate of inflation.[22] More generally, any national policy that would unilaterally raise taxes on capital incomes or reduce the expected rate of return on investments would now be punished by capital flight (Sinn 1993).[23]

At the same time, the liberalization of markets for goods and services was pushed forward by the progress of GATT and WTO negotiations in reducing tariffs and quantitative restrictions world-wide (Hoekman and Kostecki 1995) and by the spread of deregulation and privatization policies from the United States and Britain to the rest of the OECD world. Within the European Community, finally, even the remaining legal barriers protecting national economies were being abolished by the successful drive to complete the 'internal market' by the end of 1992. In short, the territorial state again lost control over its economic boundaries. Once the transnational reintegration of the markets for capital, goods, and services had surpassed a certain threshold, some observers concluded that, regretfully, 'Polanyi's Great Transformation was over' (Cerny 1994: 339), while others hailed the arrival of the 'century of globalization', in which public policy would no longer be able to counteract market forces (Giersch 1997).

At any rate, interventionist policies have become more difficult and costly at the national level—which is not to say that they are now impossible. For a while, at any rate, the

[22] Keynesian full-employment policy could thus no longer rely on the support of national monetary policy. If it was still applied at all, its full burden had to be carried by fiscal policy—which was not only less effective in economic terms but would, at high real interest rates, soon become prohibitively expensive.

[23] Conversely, national monetary policy does have the power to attract capital, by setting national interest rates above the international level. But in doing so, it will raise the exchange rate, which decreases the international competitiveness of the national economy.

'power resources of the labour movement' (Korpi 1983), and, more generally, the political forces supporting the post-war class compromise, were, and may still be, strong enough to defend existing entitlements and to resist the dismantling of the welfare state (Pierson 1994; Garrett 1995a; 1998). But even under the most auspicious political circumstances, resistance comes at considerable economic cost. Once the territorial state has lost, or given up, the capacity to control capital transfers, attempts to increase taxes on capital incomes and business profits are likely to reduce the tax base; and once the state has given up control over the boundaries of markets for goods and services, it can no longer make sure that all competing suppliers will be subject to the same regulatory regime. Thus, if now the costs of regulation or of collective bargaining are increased unilaterally within a member state, they can no longer be passed on to consumers, who are now free to turn to foreign sources.[24] Instead, and *ceteris paribus*, imports will increase in that state, exports decrease, profits will fall, investment decline, and firms will go bankrupt or move production to more benign locations.

Moreover, since the exit options of national firms, and the competitiveness of foreign suppliers, are also affected by the regulatory and tax policies of other governments, and by the strategies of unions in other countries, national govern-

---

[24] In theory, they could still be passed on to consumers through a devaluation of the national currency. However, regulations and wage settlements tend to affect specific branches of industry, rather than the economy as a whole. The loss of competitiveness may thus not be general enough to be fully compensated (from the point of view of the affected industry) by automatic adjustments of the exchange rate. Moreover, under the conditions of global currency speculation, export competitiveness is no longer the most important factor determining exchange rates. In addition, an independent central bank whose primary goal is price stability is perfectly capable of stabilizing the exchange rate at a higher level than would be justified by the international competitiveness of the national economy.

ments and unions now must compete with other locations for mobile factors of production. This 'competition among systems of regulation' seems to have the characteristics of a Prisoner's Dilemma in which all competing countries are tempted to make larger concessions to capital and business interests than they would otherwise have preferred. If the existing level of social protection is nevertheless to be maintained, a greater share of the cost must be borne by workers and consumers. Thus, the need to retain or attract mobile capital and business, and to maintain the international competitiveness of the national economy, has obvious and significant consequences for distribution. Capital incomes have risen, and income from labour has fallen behind, while governments everywhere had to shift the tax burden from mobile to relatively immobile factors—i.e. primarily onto wage incomes and consumer spending (Sinn 1993; Steinmo 1994). In short, the post-war politico-economic regimes and the welfare state are under siege even where they are still being defended (Canova 1994; Freeman 1995*a*; Pierson 1996).

In principle, this is a general problem that is felt not only in Western Europe, but in all industrialized countries—in the United States as well as in Japan or in South Korea—and which is usually discussed as a consequence of economic 'globalization'. It is particularly acute, however, within the European Union where economic integration has progressed much further, and where firms are now legally and effectively free to shop for the most attractive location of production without any constraints on their access to the former home market, and without any fear that, at some time in the future, their calculations could be upset by the imposition of 'anti-dumping levies' or by varieties of non-tariff barriers that may still be employed under the free-trade regime of the World Trade Organization (WTO). Thus, as EU member states have completely lost the option of discriminating in favour of domestic producers (Kapteyn 1996), their capacity to defend existing patterns of national policy is reduced to a much greater degree than is generally implied by the pressures of global economic competition. These tighter constraints result from the legal force of 'negative integration' in the European Community which will be discussed in the following chapter.

CHAPTER 2

Negative and Positive Integration

After the Second World War, the reintegration of European national economies into a larger, transnational context proceeded at two levels, global and regional. At both levels, the process did not just occur, but was driven by the explicit, and at times highly controversial, policy choices of the governments involved. Some of these were taken unilaterally, as was true of the early decisions by some countries to make their currencies freely convertible, and to abolish capital export controls. Others were taken jointly, but under the compulsion of uncontrollable external pressures, as was true in the early 1970s of the departure from the Bretton Woods regime of fixed exchange rates (Kapstein 1994). But by and large the economic fragmentation of the early post-war years was overcome through two parallel processes of collective decision-making. One, proceeding under American leadership through a series of GATT negotiations, aimed at the establishment of a world-wide free-trade regime; the economic goal of the other one was regional integration in (Western) Europe. Even though this book focuses on the political implications of European integration, the economic 'globalization' resulting from the first of these processes constitutes an important, and dynamically changing, background condition which needs to be kept in mind in all accounts of the political economy of European integration.

[43]

2.1 PURPOSES OF REGIONAL INTEGRATION

European integration was initiated for political, rather than economic reasons—by France to achieve a more permanent control of the German potential than had been possible after the First World War, by Germany to escape the fate of an outcast nation (Urwin 1991). But when, after the failure of the European Defence Community, it was accepted that for the time being progress could only be achieved on the economic front, the logic of regional economic integration came to dominate the political agenda, and to drive the further institutional evolution.

Considering only the economic dimension, integration will enlarge the size of product markets, allowing producers to capture the efficiency gains associated with economies of scale. By the same token, however, less efficient producers will suffer from the opening of their home markets to more efficient foreign competitors. By contrast, consumers will generally benefit from more efficient production, more intense competition, and the welfare gains ascribed to free trade by the economic theory of comparative advantage (Norrie et al. 1986: ch. 16; Emerson et al. 1988; Smith and Venables 1988; Bakhoven 1990). Thus, from the perspective of economic theory, free trade is always justified by the benefits accruing to consumer interests.[1] From a political perspective, however, the conclusion may be more ambiguous. Individuals and households will be affected by economic change not only as consumers, but also as producers. Thus, if benefits to consumers should be achieved at the expense of producers,[2]

---

[1] From a purely economic perspective, regional integration is, of course, only a second-best solution. The ideal is world-wide free trade.

[2] Analytically, the category of producers would include capital owners as well as workers. But since the minimal rate of return on capital investments is assured by the exit options of the capital market, the squeeze on producers is mainly felt by workers.

they may be more intensely affected by sectoral and regional dislocations of production, and by intensified competition, than by gains in their roles as consumers.[3] Governments, at any rate, must politically respond to both types of economic interests, and to a great many non-economic concerns as well.

2.1.1 Stages of Economic Integration

In the theory of economic policy, it is usual to distinguish between 'negative' and 'positive integration' (Tinbergen 1965). Both terms, it is important to note, refer not to economic processes as such, but to government policy aimed at enlarging the economic space beyond existing national boundaries. In this sense, *negative integration* refers to the removal of tariffs, quantitative restrictions, and other barriers to trade or obstacles to free and undistorted competition. *Positive integration*, by contrast, refers to the reconstruction of a system of economic regulation at the level of the larger economic unit. The distinction is not completely synonymous with a second one between 'market-making' and 'market-correcting' policy interventions. While all measures of negative integration should probably be classified as being market-making, measures of positive integration may be either market-making (e.g. if divergent national product standards are being 'harmonized' in order to eliminate existing non-tariff barriers to trade) or market-correcting (e.g. process-oriented regulations of working conditions or pollution control). This second distinction marks the front line of ideological conflict between anti-interventionist (e.g. neoliberal) and interventionist (e.g. social-democratic or Keynesian)

---

[3] The relationship is not strictly negative, since gains in the efficiency of production may also improve the quality of working life.

theorists, political parties, and interest groups. From an anti-interventionist point of view, what matters is negative integration, whereas positive integration is acceptable only in so far as it serves market-making purposes (e.g. through the adoption and implementation of rules of undistorted competition). From an interventionist perspective, by contrast, negative integration should be considered problematical unless it is accompanied by the creation of political capacities for market-correcting positive integration.

With regard to the intensity of integration, economists distinguish between the Free-Trade Area, the Customs Union, the Common Market, and the Economic Union (Courchene 1983; Norrie et al. 1986: ch. 16; El-Agraa 1990). In a *Free-Trade Area*, the participating governments merely agree to remove customs duties and quantitative restrictions on imports and exports between their territories, while each remains free to maintain or impose its own barriers against non-members.

If the goal is a universal regime like the GATT, free-trade rules may perhaps represent a potentially stable end state.[4] In projects of regional integration, however, it will be difficult to prevent goods imported into one member state from moving to other member territories. Thus regional free-trade regimes will find themselves under some pressure to develop into a *Customs Union* in which tariff barriers and quantitative restrictions to trade with non-member states are harmonized among the members. In the European Community, that stage was reached by 1968 (Moussis 1994: ch. 1).

The Customs Union still leaves most non-tariff barriers between the member economies in place, whereas a *Common*

---

[4] Nevertheless, recent rounds of GATT negotiations also achieved progress in the elimination of non-tariff barriers, especially with regard to services.

Market would assure the free movement of goods, services, capital, and labour across territorial borders either by *removing* national regulations and practices that have the effect of discriminating against foreign products or foreign service providers, or by *harmonizing* national regulations that would otherwise distort competition. In the European Community, that stage was reached with the completion of the internal market at the end of 1992 (Moussis 1994: ch. 2). Finally, in an *Economic and Monetary Union*, the member states would also agree to adopt a common currency and common policies with regard to economic matters in order to eliminate the frictions and disruptions resulting from divergent national interventions in the common market. Quite obviously, reaching this final stage is more important for political actors that are convinced of the need for policy interventions in the capitalist economy, while neoliberal economists and political parties could well content themselves with the completion of a common market.

2.1.2 The Political Dynamics of Economic Integration

If countries joining in regional integration should differ originally with regard to their political preferences for economic intervention, that difference by itself can become a powerful force pushing for further integration. Assume, for example, a free-trade area with some 'interventionist' member countries that have high tariff walls, powerful unions, and high levels of regulation regarding product quality, work safety, pollution control, and social security, and with some 'neoliberal' member countries that have low or non-existent external barriers, weak unions, and low levels of product- and process-related regulation. Assuming that all other conditions are about equal, this free-trade area will need to cope with three types of problems.

[47]

The first has already been alluded to. If external tariffs should differ significantly, third countries would direct their exports to the low-tariff countries, from where they would then find their way into all other member states. This would leave high-tariff countries with the presumably unattractive choice either of seeing their tariff protection disappear as a consequence of trade dislocation, or of establishing internal tariff barriers against third-country products—which would partly frustrate the intentions associated with the free-trade area. As a consequence, regional free-trade areas among countries with significantly different levels of external protection are pushed toward adopting common policies with regard to the outside world—i.e. toward becoming at least a customs union. But that would then require resolution of the conflict of interest between high- and low-tariff countries, and even if that conflict were resolved, it would leave the high-tariff countries with a lesser capacity to vary their levels of protection in response to sectoral differences or to changes over time.

The second problem arises if the members of the customs union have significantly different levels (or types) of product-quality regulation. If each country remains free to apply its own product standards to national as well as to imported products, producers would still need to develop and produce different products for nationally fragmented markets. Thus, to capture the potential efficiencies of economic integration, members would need to move forward to a common market that was no longer fragmented by non-tariff barriers. This could be achieved in two different ways. From a neoliberal perspective, the proper method would be *mutual recognition*, according to which products which are lawful in their country of origin could be freely traded in all member countries. The resulting 'regulatory competition' would, and should, then be decided by the choice of consumers among products produced under different standards. From a more interventionist point of view, by contrast, the proper method would be *harmonization*, and each country should remain free to apply its own product standards as long as agreement on common standards was not yet achieved.

Regardless of how it is attained, from a neoliberal point of view most legitimate aspirations of economic integration are realized with the completion of the common market,[5] and further moves toward positive integration are generally considered unnecessary and dangerous (Basedow 1992; Mestmäcker 1992). From an interventionist perspective, by contrast, the common market as such appears as a constraint that reduces the capacity of national political systems to pursue democratically legitimized policy goals. It is likely to undermine existing product regulations under a rule of mutual recognition, and even if product rules are harmonized, the competition among national regulatory regimes will threaten the viability of national attempts to regulate the processes of capitalist production and maintain welfare-state redistribution. Thus, the more negative integration advances, the more political preferences for market-correcting interventions appear to depend on positive integration—that is on the adoption of uniform regulations at the regional level. But since, as I will argue immediately below, the institutional capacity for negative integration is stronger than the capacity for positive integration, interventionist policies, and the interests they could serve, are systematically disadvantaged in the process of European integration.

[5] Going further toward a monetary union would reduce transaction costs—but under conditions of freely convertible currencies, and under the assumption of well-functioning financial markets, these should not be a major concern from the neoliberal perspective.

2.2 THE SUPRANATIONAL EFFECTIVENESS
OF NEGATIVE INTEGRATION

The process of European integration is characterized by a fundamental asymmetry which was first pointed out by Joseph Weiler (1982), who described it as a dualism between supranational European law and intergovernmental European policy-making. Weiler was also right in criticizing political scientists for having too long focused only on aspects of intergovernmental negotiations while ignoring (or, at least, not taking seriously enough) the establishment, by judge-made law, of a European legal order that takes precedence over national law (Weiler 1994). This omission was all the more critical since it also kept political scientists from recognizing the parallel between Weiler's legal dualism and the economic dualism of 'negative' and 'positive integration'.

The point is that so far the main beneficiary of supranational European law has been negative integration. Its basic rules were already contained in the 'primary law' of the Treaties of Rome which contained explicit commitments to reduce and abolish tariffs and quantitative restrictions on trade between member states as well as the rudimentary principles of a European law of free and undistorted market competition. From this foundation, liberalization could be extended, without much political attention, through interventions of the European Commission against infringements of Treaty obligations, and through the decisions and preliminary rulings of the European Court of Justice. By contrast, positive integration depends upon the agreement of national governments in the Council of Ministers and, increasingly, on the agreement of the European Parliament as well (in which the 'diffuse' interests of consumers and environmental protection have gained a strong foothold—Pollack 1997a); it is thus subject to the combined impediments facing consensual intergovernmental and pluralist policy-making. This fundamental institutional difference is sufficient to explain the frequently deplored asymmetry between negative and positive integration in EC policy-making (Kapteyn 1991; Merkel 1993*b*).

But how was this institutional advantage achieved? In the abstract, it is true, the desirability of economic integration was not in dispute. The basic commitment to create a 'Common Market' was shared by the governments that were parties to the Treaties and by the national parliaments that ratified these agreements. It found its legal expression in Treaty provisions which were clear with regard to the commitment to a (gradual) elimination of tariffs and quantitative restrictions on imports (Arts. 12–17, 30–5 TEC). By contrast, the prohibitions against national regulations operating as non-tariff barriers (i.e. 'all measures having equivalent effect' to quantitative restrictions, Art. 30 TEC) were not only worded less precisely, but also qualified by the numerous and in part rather vague 'public-order' exceptions of Art. 36 TEC which could only be overcome through 'positive' harmonization decisions by the Council. Similarly, the provisions of competition law were relatively precise with regard to private enterprises (Arts. 85–7 TEC), but less clear and shot through with important exceptions with regard to the prohibition against competition-distorting state subsidies (Arts. 92–4 TEC). Even more ambivalent is the wording of Art. 90 TEC which, in paragraph 1, obliges member states to respect the rules of competition law with regard to 'public undertakings and undertakings to which Member States grant special or exclusive rights', but in its paragraph 2 exempts 'undertakings entrusted with the operation of services of general economic interest or having the character of a revenue-producing monopoly'. If these were to be touched at all, one could have thought that any moves toward liberalization would depend on 'political' action by the Council of

Ministers—just as political action had been necessary to bring about the common market in agriculture that had been ordained in Arts. 38–47 TEC, and as it was explicitly required for the creation of a common transport policy (Arts. 75–84 TEC), or for the liberalization of the markets for services (Art. 63 TEC) and for capital (Art. 69 TEC).

However, after the elimination of tariffs and quantitative restrictions, and after the fight over agriculture that had almost destroyed the European Community (Webber 1997), political action had slowed down. As a consequence of the 'Luxembourg compromise' of 1966, even market-making Council decisions continued to depend on unanimous agreement,[6] and they were often blocked by conflicts of interest between the more and less interventionist member states. Thus, with the exception of the Common Agricultural Policy, European economic integration seemed to stagnate at the level of a customs union, and the Treaty provisions against non-tariff barriers and competition-distorting state action more or less lay dormant until the mid-1980s.

2.2.1 Direct Effect and Supremacy

There was no stagnation in the evolution of the legal system of the Community, however. In contrast to the GATT, where the enforcement of treaty provisions is ultimately left

[6] Actually, the precise wording, and the intended meaning, of the accord of 29 Jan. 1996 had not implied unanimity, but merely a commitment of all member governments to search for consensual solutions before, ultimately, resorting to majority decisions (Lahr 1983). Subsequent practice, however, and the announcement of the French government, that it would vote with any government that claimed to be affected in its 'very important national interests', amounted to a *de facto* requirement of unanimous decisions— which then was formally relaxed in some areas related to the completion of the internal market by the Single European Act of 1986 (Teasdale 1993).

to the retaliatory action of the injured states (Hoekman and Kostecki 1995), the EC Treaty had from the beginning provided for its own enforcement system. The Commission had a general mandate to identify and prosecute Treaty infringements, and the European Court of Justice was given the power to issue legally binding judgments, and it now is even authorized to impose penalties, against member states violating their Treaty commitments (Art. 171 TEC). Moreover, and in fact more important, the Court will issue preliminary rulings on the authoritative interpretation of Community law at the request of the ordinary courts of member states (Art. 177 TEC). From this procedural competence, it was only a small logical step—which the Court was quick to take[7]—to the conclusion that at least some of the law of the Treaty was meant to have 'direct effect' as the law of the land within member states. Or how else could questions of European law become decisive in ordinary proceedings before national courts? But this seemingly logical step had far-reaching consequences. It liberated European law from the control that national governments would otherwise exercise over the domestic implementation of international agreements.

If 'direct effect' was the foot in the door, the gates were thrown wide open by the doctrine of 'supremacy' which eliminated the control of national parliaments and constitutional courts as well. Here, the logical step that the Court needed to take was larger. If (some) European law was to have direct effect, clearly its relation to national law had to be determined. Since the Treaty had been ratified by the legislatures in all member states, it was plausible to argue that its provisions, *given their direct effect*, should override *prior* acts of national legislation. By the same logic, however, European

---

[7] Case 26-62, *Van Gend and Loos* v. *Nederlands Administratie der Belastingen* (1963).

law would have to give way to all acts of national legislation *subsequent* to the ratification decision. As a consequence, the body of European law would become a patchwork, with some provisions applicable in some member states, and others applicable elsewhere. The Court avoided this practical difficulty by postulating the supremacy of directly effective Treaty provisions over *all* national law, prior or subsequent, administrative, statutory, or constitutional.[8] Subsequently the doctrine was extended to all varieties of European law[9]— including Council directives not yet transformed into national law by the national legislature (on the basis of which private parties can now claim damages from their shirking governments).[10]

From a political point of view, the most important effect of the combined doctrines of direct effect and supremacy has been the constitutionalization of competition law. Direct effect opened the way to the development of a vigorous European competition law which, given the low emphasis on anti-trust rules in the law of most member states, was driven mainly by the contributions, and the neoliberal conceptual framework, of German specialists in the law and economics of competition (von der Groeben 1996). The supremacy doctrine then had the effect of placing their conclusions beyond even the control of parliamentary super-majorities at the national level.

2.2.2 The Constitutionalization of Competition Law

By championing the primacy of European law, the Court created a logical contradiction within national constitutional

---

[8] Case 6-64, *Flaminio Costa* v. *Enel* (1964).

[9] Case 106-77, *Amministrazione delle Finanze* v. *Simmenthal* (1978).

[10] Joined Cases 6 and 9-90, *Francovich and Others* v. *Italy* (1992).

law: how could legislation based on a treaty, ratified by an act of the national legislature, override national constitutions that could not have been amended by the same legislature in the same procedure? This contradiction has been of particular concern to the Federal Constitutional Court in Germany,[11] and it seems fair to say that it has not yet found a satisfactory resolution. What matters from a practical point of view, however, is the fact that, by and large, national courts and their interlocutors have been willing to go along with the doctrines of direct effect and of supremacy, of European over national law (Weiler 1992; Burley and Mattli 1993; but see Golub 1996a; Caruso 1997). The political significance of this acceptance becomes clearer when it is realized that it also implies an effective monopoly of the European Court of Justice in the *substantive interpretation* of European law.

The political importance of interpretation became most obvious with regard to Art. 36 TEC, which exempts from the prohibition of non-tariff barriers (Art. 30 TEC) restrictions on imports that are justified on grounds of 'public morality, public policy or public security', or that serve the protection of 'health and life of humans, animals or plants' and so on. Given the wide range of these exemptions, who should be the ultimate judge of whether a particular regulation does in fact serve one of the public-interest purposes allowed in Art. 36 TEC? Within a national context, for instance, the Supreme Court of the United States has consistently refused to

[11] The Bundesverfassungsgericht did accept the doctrines of direct effect and supremacy, and also the binding effect of the ECJ's preliminary rulings with regard to Council directives that had not yet been transformed into national law (BVerfGE 75, 223, 1987). However, in its famous *Solange* decisions, the German court first asserted, and later suspended, its own final authority to determine the compatibility of European law with the basic individual rights protected by the German constitution (BVerfGE 37, 271, 1974 and BVerfGE 73, 339, 1986).

second-guess the 'political branches' of government on the plausibility of the means–end assumptions underlying otherwise permissible measures (Scharpf 1966). But since the exemptions of Art. 36 TEC are qualified by the further proviso that national regulations must not 'constitute a means of arbitrary discrimination or a disguised restriction on trade between Member States', judicial deference to the judgement of *national* legislatures could, again, raise the spectre of fragmented markets.

Under the circumstances, the European Court did not hesitate to rely on its own factual judgement to invalidate a particularly far-fetched justification in the landmark case of *Cassis de Dijon* (120-78, 1979).[12] In doing so, it not only asserted its competence to assess the intrinsic reasonableness of all national health, safety, or environmental product regulations that could have a negative impact on free trade,[13] but it also announced the new rule of *mutual recognition*: whenever national regulations did not serve a valid public-interest purpose (as defined by the Court), there was no need for harmonization since products lawfully marketed in one member state must be admitted in all member states of the Community. By judicial fiat, in other words, the freedom to sell and to consume had achieved constitutional protection against the political judgement of democratically legitimized legislatures.

That is surely a remarkable achievement, whose legitimacy is still debated in legal theory (Friedbacher 1996; Maduro 1997). Even in the Federal Republic of Germany, where the

---

[12] The German government had defended the exclusion of the French liqueur as a public-health measure, arguing that since its alcohol content was *lower* than the standard defined for liqueurs in Germany, it might become an 'entry drug' for unwary consumers.

[13] For a discussion of recent decisions that suggests that the ECJ is indeed becoming sensitive to the 'functional' limitations of its fact-finding and law-making competencies, see Maduro (1997).

notion of an 'economic constitution' enshrining the principles of a 'social market economy'[14] has been most influential, these propositions never achieved constitutional status (Basedow 1992). Instead, the German Constitutional Court consistently emphasized the 'neutrality of the Basic Law in matters of economic policy'.[15] In Germany, therefore, economic freedom is protected against state intervention only within the general framework of basic human and civil rights, and the goals of competition policy have no higher constitutional status than all other legitimate purposes of public policy. Accordingly, market-creating as well as market-correcting policy proposals must compete on the same constitutional footing, and—witness the uneven history of cartel legislation and practice—they have to cope with the same difficulties of finding political support in the face of ubiquitous opposition. This is also true in other member states of the European Community where, generally speaking, public policy is even less constrained by considerations of the 'economic-constitution' type.[16]

It does not follow from the text of the Treaties of Rome or from their genesis that the European Community was meant to abolish this constitutional parity between the protection of

[14] In any case, the concept was defined, by its original promoter, as the combination of the 'principle of market freedom with that of social compensation' (Müller-Armack 1996: 243), rather than as the maximization of free competition.

[15] See e.g. BVerfGE 4, 7, 1954; BVerfGE 25, 1, 1968; BVerfGE 30, 292, 1971; BVerfGE 50, 290, 1978.

[16] As far as I am aware, the only exception to that rule was, for a few decades, the doctrine of 'economic due process' which (together with the 'negative commerce clause') the US Supreme Court had used, from the beginning of this century until the 'New Deal Revolution' in the mid-1930s, to protect free enterprise against efforts of either the federal government or the states to regulate the use of child labour, or the working time of women, or any other type of social legislation (Schubert 1960: ch. 8; Ehmke 1961).

economic freedom and market-correcting intervention (VerLoren van Themaat 1987; Joerges 1991; 1994*a*; von der Groeben 1992; Ehlermann 1995). Nevertheless, as a consequence of the supremacy of European law, the four economic freedoms, and the injunctions against distortions of competition, have in fact gained constitutional force *vis-à-vis* the member states (Gerber 1988; Behrens 1994; Mestmäcker 1994: 270).

2.2.3 Challenging the Mixed Economy

The political implications were not particularly acute as long as the Commission and the Court were mainly proceeding against non-tariff barriers to the trade of goods, against violations of competition rules in market sectors, and against the discrimination of foreign competitors. In all European countries, however, there was and still is a wide range of goods and service production, and of infrastructure functions, that is generally (i.e. without specifically discriminating against foreign producers) more or less exempted from market competition. In the political-economy literature of the 1960s and 1970s, these areas have been described as being characteristic of 'mixed economies', combining market elements and intense state intervention. In the older terminology of the Anglo-American common law, they are treated as businesses 'affected by a public interest'; in France they are considered part of the 'service public'. In Germany, the cartel law recognizes them as 'Ausnahmebereiche', and in our own research, we have described them as 'staatsnahe Sektoren' in which the involvement of the state is more extensive or more intense than is true of the economy in general (Mayntz and Scharpf 1995*b*).

In the mixed economy, forms of state involvement did and

do vary widely among countries, and within countries among sectors—ranging from the direct provision of services by state agencies through public enterprises, licensed private monopolies, publicly sanctioned cartels, or intensively regulated professional services, all the way to the mere subsidization of production or consumption. Substantively, countries also differ in what is, and is not, included in the mixed economy. In general however, the category used to encompass the functions of education, basic research, radio and TV, health care, old-age pensions, telecommunications, rail, air, and road transport, energy supply, banking, stock exchanges, and agriculture.

From a neoliberal point of view, these exemptions from the norm of competitive markets have always been regarded with suspicion. At the national level, nevertheless, their legal status was secure. Even in Germany, where neoliberal doctrines had the greatest influence, cartel law never had a higher constitutional standing than the legislation organizing the telephone system as a public monopoly, regulating the cartel conditions of the road haulage industry, or subsidizing coal mines through a surcharge on the price of electricity. Even if such laws precluded, limited, or distorted free market competition, their legitimacy derived from the same political judgements of parliamentary majorities on which the cartel law depended as well.

If this was true in Germany, it was even more true in all other member states of the European Community which, generally, had placed much less emphasis on the legal protection of free competition. In short: nowhere within the member states of the European Community would it have been possible to launch a successful *legal* attack on the privileged status of the *service public* or of the *staatsnahe Sektoren* on the grounds that the authorizing legislation was in violation of competition law. But this victory, which had always escaped competition lawyers at the national level, was finally achieved through the constitutionalization of European competition law (Cox 1996).

The victory, however, had been long in coming, and it is still far from complete. It was only in the mid–1980s, when the political push to complete the 'internal market' was already under way, and when changes in technology and international competition had begun to erode the economic viability of national telecommunications monopolies (Schneider 1995), that the Commission initiated proceedings against countries that allowed their PTT monopolies to exclude third-party suppliers of terminal equipment and value-added services. Encouraged by the assent of the Court in individual cases, it then chose to employ the most dramatic weapon in its arsenal—'Commission directives' which, under Art. 90 III TEC, can be adopted by a majority of commissioners without agreement of the Council—to abolish all remaining PTT monopolies in the markets for terminal equipment and value-added services. Against many expectations,[17] the Court agreed once more.[18] Nevertheless, as Susanne Schmidt (1998) has shown, Commission directives remain an exceptional instrument that the Commission will use only under favourable political circumstances.

There is no such hesitation, however, in the Commission's use of its powers, under Arts. 89 II and 90 III TEC, to issue 'decisions' in individual cases against the violation of competition rules, or to initiate Court proceedings against national infringements of Treaty obligations under Art. 169 TEC. For all of these actions, a Council vote is not required, and the

[17] The Commission's own legal service had had serious misgivings about the use of this form of legislation, and the Advocate General had argued against it before the Court.

[18] Case 202/88, *French Republic and Commission of the European Communities* (1991) and cases 271/90, 281/90, and 289/90 (1992).

national governments affected are only involved in the role of respondents in a legal proceeding. In this fashion, the Commission has been able to advance the liberalization of one area of *service public* after another, from telecommunications, to air transport and airport operations, to road haulage, postal services, the energy market, and a number of other services (S. Schmidt 1997*b*).

By the logic of these decisions, no area of *service public* is now beyond the challenge of European competition law. Given the great institutional diversity among member states, it is always possible to argue that existing national arrangements are discriminating against actual or potential private competitors from abroad: just as the placement monopoly of the German Labour Administration was required to allow the competition of private manpower placement services,[19] so the privileged position of public radio and television[20] (Kleinsteuber and Rossmann 1994), and the existence of state guarantees for deposits in public banks,[21] are challenged by private competitors as being in violation of EC competition law. By the same logic, private schools and universities could now demand to compete under equal conditions with public education systems; commercial health maintenance organizations could challenge the public health systems in the Scandinavian countries and Britain as well as the systems of compulsory health insurance on the European continent; and the same demand might be addressed by private pension funds against pension systems financed from general tax revenue or from compulsory insurance schemes.

I am not arguing that all of this would be horrible; some

---

[19] Case 41/90, *Hoefner and Macroton GmbH* (1991).

[20] Case 260/89, *ERT and Dimotiki Etairia and Others* (1991).

[21] At the Amsterdam Summit, the German government, under pressure from the *Länder*, has been able to achieve some support for the status of public banks. This will be discussed in Ch. 5, below.

such changes might in fact be desirable or even inevitable on their merits. Nor am I arguing that all of this is going to happen soon. Art. 90 TEC had existed for almost thirty years before the Commission and the Court began seriously to enter the *service public* field, and it is obvious that both are proceeding with caution when they sense broad political resistance (S. Schmidt 1997*b*; 1998).[22] Nevertheless, European competition law is a 'fleet in being' that will affect national policy choices through its anticipation and its influence on the domestic balance of political forces even when direct intervention is avoided.

2.2.4 The Political Costs of Negative Integration

The single-minded pursuit of market liberalization tends to ignore the fact that the institutions of the mixed economy were created to solve problems which, at the time, were thought sufficiently salient to justify the departure from pure market provision. In some areas, these justifications could be equated with the need to correct specific types of 'market failures', as these are defined in welfare-theoretic analyses that start from the premiss that the market should have its way whenever a market solution is logically possible. In democratic practice, however, political intervention has never been limited to the correction of market failures as defined by welfare economics or by the new 'constitutional political economy' (Brennan and Buchanan 1985). Other reasons for state intervention that were considered politically legitimate have generally included considerations of military efficiency or of state revenue, the security of critical supplies in times of war and international crises, and, most importantly, political

---

[22] See also Ch. 5, below.

commitments to solidaristic redistribution among genera-
tions and social classes, and to equality among subnational
regions with regard to basic services, infrastructure facilities,
and economic opportunities. Still other concerns were
thought to justify the financial support of independent public-service radio and television networks in order to protect
the integrity of mass communication against political as well
as commercial manipulation.

Who Should Decide?

It is often argued, and it may indeed be true, that some of
these concerns have lost theoretical plausibility or political
salience as a consequence of technological advances or of
changes in the international economic environment.[23] Nevertheless, the issue remains who should be deciding about the
desirability, the timing, and the direction of changes in the
regulatory regimes of what used to be the mixed economy:
national parliaments, the Council of Ministers, or the Commission and the European Court? Historically, there is no
question that neither the governments negotiating the Treaties of Rome nor the parliaments ratifying them had any
intention to use European competition law to challenge the
existence of *service public* functions in the member states of
the Community. In fact, Art. 90 II TEC contains language
which suggests exactly the opposite. Moreover, as I pointed out above, when it was foreseen that creating an integrated market would be desirable in sectors that were under
intense state influence—as was true in agriculture (Arts.
38–47 TEC), capital markets (Arts. 67–73 h TEC), and

---

[23] This seems to be true in the case of telecommunications (Schneider
1995; S. Schmidt 1997*b*). Also, in the case of radio and television, the
scarcity of available frequencies, which was *one of the reasons* for public
regulation, has been alleviated by satellite and digital transmission.

transportation (Arts. 75–84 TEC)—the Treaty had explicitly provided for integration through political decisions by the Council. Nevertheless, when agreement on a common transport regime could not be achieved, the Commission and the Court proceeded on their own to liberalize the sector (Héritier 1997).

From a democratic perspective, this assumption of law-making powers by the Commission and the Court in politically highly salient policy areas must appear problematic. It is also true, however, that the Continental, and certainly the German, legal tradition is generally less willing to respect the priority of democratically legitimized legislation over the law-making functions of courts and academic lawyers than is true in American constitutional theory and practice (Hand 1960; Bickel 1962; Scharpf 1966; 1970b; Ackerman 1992; Komesar 1994). In any case, public concern over the democratic legitimacy of European policy choices was long in coming and, ironically, when it did finally arise, it tended to focus mainly on the law-making functions of the Council (where qualified-majority voting was reinstalled by the Single European Act) rather than on decisions by the Commission or the Court.

Why Did Governments Acquiesce?

Why national governments should have acquiesced in this expansion of judicial legislation has become an interesting test case for competing approaches to integration theory. Within a *liberal intergovernmentalist* framework, which treats nation states, or national governments, as the only relevant actors not only in international relations, but also in the process of European integration, Geoffrey Garrett (1992; 1995b) interprets the case law of the European Court of Justice as the focal point of a latent consensus among national governments, and in particular of France and Germany, whereas Andrew

Moravcsik (1993; 1994) emphasizes the benefits national governments derive from the fact that some classes of difficult decisions (and the blame for them) could be left to the responsibility of the Commission and the Court. The implication seems to be that if this were not so, governments would have been able to prevent outcomes which they considered undesirable.[24]

That interpretation is challenged by authors committed to the *neofunctionalist* or *supranationalist* framework. Burley and Mattli (1993), for instance, start from the observation that in many cases governments have fought hard to prevent the outcomes imposed by the Court.[25] Rejecting the intergovernmentalist interpretation, they emphasize the active role of the Commission and of the Court whose policy choices are injected into national legal systems through the gateway of applications by national courts for 'preliminary rulings'

---

[24] It should be said, however, that Moravcsik's framework of 'liberal intergovernmentalism' is mainly intended to structure the explanation of 'celebrated intergovernmental bargains' in the history of European integration. Thus, by its own terms, the application of the framework to 'everyday decisions' must make use of a 'delegation' module that allows for the possibility that national governments (modelled as multiple 'principals') may have difficulty in controlling the Commission and the Court (modelled as self-interested 'agents' (see also Pollack 1997a)). Hence Moravcsik (1993) does acknowledge the possibility that national governments might not be able to control the evolution of European law in all respects, but he considers this an exception of minor importance.

[25] Taking the *Cassis* case as their major example, however, Burley and Mattli have weakened their critical argument. Any reasonable reading of the intergovernmentalist position would have to allow for a distinction between levels of rules, or between a rule and its application (Kiser and Ostrom 1982): the fact that a government, when caught in a transgression, objects to the *application* of a rule does not prove that it also objects to the rule itself. Instead, I am arguing that the judicial expansion of negative integration was achieved under institutional conditions in which the *formulation of the rule* itself was largely beyond the control of national governments.

[65]

under Art. 177 TEC. Once they have become part of the national law that is applied by national courts, these policy choices are protected by the relative autonomy of the legal system and its effectiveness as a 'mask and shield' that prevents direct political intervention against the outcomes of legal processes.[26] The implication, then, is that it is the cognitive orientations and policy preferences of supranational actors, rather than of national governments, that one must examine in order to explain European policy outcomes.

For empirical research over a variety of policy areas, however, it seems that neither of these across-the-board generalizations will be of much help (Schmidt 1996). In our own work, we prefer to use the framework of 'actor-centred institutionalism' (Mayntz and Scharpf 1995a; Scharpf 1997a) as a general guide for reconstructing policy interactions under the specific enabling and constraining conditions of different institutional settings. This framework avoids a-priori assumptions about the relative importance of specific classes of actors, allowing for the possibility that in addition to national governments other corporate actors may play a significant role in European decision processes. Among these, the Commission and the Court do indeed occupy institutionally privileged positions from which they are able to employ important action resources in order to achieve goals that are not only defined by institutional self-interest and normative mandates, but may also be strongly shaped by the 'ideas' prevailing in a particular 'epistemic community' (Haas 1992)—e.g. by the doctrines of neoliberal competition law which seem to have played a large role in the history of European integration.[27]

But though the Commission and the Court, and increasingly the European Parliament, may need to be taken into

[26] See also Weiler (1992; 1994) and Mattli and Slaughter (1995).
[27] But see the cases cited in n. 18 above and in Maduro (1997).

account alongside national governments (which, in turn may need to be disaggregated to account for the influence of individual ministries or of certain subnational actors), their relative importance in the constellation of strategic actors depends upon, and varies with, the specific rules of the institutional setting within which the interaction must take place. This suggests that it should be useful to distinguish empirically between those areas where European policy must be defined by regulations and directives requiring agreement of the Council of Ministers, and other areas, where the Commission is formally entitled to act without involving the Council, and where its success as a definer of European policy depends ultimately on the approval of the European Court of Justice.

In the latter area, intergovernmentalist assumptions seem to be less plausible than in the former. But that does not mean that the role of national governments could be ignored. Take the example mentioned above, of the Commission's anomalous power to issue directives of general application under Art. 90 III TEC without any formal involvement of the Council. These 'Commission directives' have played a large role in the comparatively rapid liberalization of telecommunications markets in Europe. However, as Susanne Schmidt (1997*b*) has shown, the Commission failed to use this power in arguably similar cases, and its practical reach seems to be limited to policy choices that are at least tacitly accepted by most member governments. The explanation requires a look into the 'black box' of the corporate actor described as 'the Commission' (Ross 1995). Whereas decisions are likely to be prepared within, and from the perspective of, a single, specialized directorate general, they must be approved by a majority of all commissioners. Among these, some may be responsible for portfolios representing conflicting interests and policy positions. In that case, the decision is likely to hinge on the votes of commissioners that have no intrinsic preference one way or another. These, however, owe their positions to their respective national governments, which also suggests that they (and the members of their *cabinets*—who are likely to be civil servants at relatively early stages in their careers) are not entirely immune to pressures exerted by their home governments in matters that do not concern their own portfolio. Hence, if a sufficient number of governments should find a proposal sufficiently obnoxious to overcome their distaste for arm-twisting, it is not unrealistic to think that this proposal may fail to find support in the full Commission.

Paradoxically, however, the directorate general that was defeated on a Commission directive may have a better chance of achieving its original purposes by way of a Council directive. The paradox is resolved by the observation that, just as member governments are able to exert ('intergovernmental') influence on members of the Commission, so the directorate in charge is able to exert ('supranational') influence on members of the Council of Ministers. The underlying mechanisms are complex and theoretically interesting: within the Commission, the Directorate in charge is less likely to be opposed by a majority of commissioners when it proposes action in individual cases, rather than directives of general application. Governments not immediately affected will either not care to intervene with 'their' commissioners or may even welcome Commission action against the protectionist practices of another state. Thus, provided that it is able to find 'good' cases,[28] the directorate is free to proceed against individual

[28] In practice, that is a very important proviso. Thus the Commission was unable to attack regional electricity monopolies in Germany directly, because suppliers in other countries were reluctant to antagonize their German counterparts, and because firms that would have liked to purchase cheaper electricity from across the border were dissuaded from legal action

countries one at a time. When it succeeds in court, however, the decision will stand as a precedent that affects expectations far beyond the case at hand. Moreover, and more important here, the government that has been enjoined from using certain restrictive practices will find that its own 'default condition' in negotiations over a Council directive has been changed (S. Schmidt 1997*a*). Once a country has been forced to open its own markets unilaterally, it cannot have an interest in allowing other countries to maintain their protectionist practices. Hence governments that were the victims of successful legal action are likely to become political allies of the Commission when a general directive subjecting all member states to the same regime is subsequently proposed to the Council. This, at any rate, has been the strategy through which liberalization in sectors such as telecommunications, air transport, road haulage, electricity, and others was ultimately achieved through Council directives, even though initially the governments opposed to liberalization could have blocked such directives (Héritier 1997; S. Schmidt 1997*b*; 1998).

The Strength of Negative Integration

Two conclusions seem to follow: first, even when negative integration must be pursued through Council directives, rather than through legal action in individual cases, the Commission remains a resourceful actor with considerable strategic advantages in a complex multi-level game that, in addition to the member state governments in the Council of Ministers, involves not only the European Parliament (with its general bias for more integration of any kind) but also the Court and those private parties who could serve as litigants in individual

by the offer of 'sweetheart deals' from their German electricity suppliers (S. Schmidt 1997*b*: ch. 4.3.4).

[69]

cases and controversies that suit the Commission's purposes. Hence appropriate explanations could neither be generally 'intergovernmentalist' nor 'supranationalist', but need to reconstruct the strategic constellations as they are defined by the institutional setting within which interactions take place.

Beyond this methodological argument, what matters here is a second, substantive conclusion. The strong strategic position of the Commission, which allows it to undermine and change the negotiation positions of national governments in the Council of Ministers, derives from its power to take legal action, without prior authorization by the Council, against the violation of Treaty obligations by member states. With few exceptions,[29] this power is limited to interventions against national barriers to free trade and mobility, and against national practices distorting market competition. Hence the mechanism described is by no means generally available for expediting all kinds of Council decisions, but is practically limited to 'market-making' Council directives that liberalize hitherto protected, cartellized, or monopolized national markets, and that force member states to allow market competition in services that had hitherto been provided by state agencies. It is, in other words, only available to support the extension of negative integration.

There are, then, powerful institutional mechanisms that have allowed the Commission and the Court of Justice continuously to expand the legal reach of negative integration without recourse to political legitimization—i.e. political legitimization that is more specific and more contemporaneous than the original agreement on the text of the Treaties or, for that matter, the willingness of new member states to sub-

---

[29] A major exception is the enforcement of gender equality under Art. 119 TEC (Ostner and Lewis 1995).

scribe to the *acquis communautaire* as a condition of entry into the Community. From an interventionist perspective, therefore, as the legal constraints of negative integration, and the economic constraints of competition in the internal market, are progressively reducing the range of national policy choices, the capacity for market-correcting measures of positive integration at the European level should also increase, if a fundamental loss of political control over the capitalist economy is to be avoided.[30]

2.3 THE WEAKNESS OF POSITIVE INTEGRATION

While negative integration could be advanced by the Commission and the Court, as it were behind the back of politically legitimized actors, measures of positive integration generally require explicit approval by the Council of Ministers and, increasingly, by the European Parliament. As a consequence, the problem-solving capacity of positive integration is limited by the need to achieve action consensus among a wide range of divergent national and group interests.

---

[30] From a neoliberal perspective, that was of course exactly the purpose of the exercise. In this view, the Community was meant to do no more than to establish and safeguard the postulates of economic freedom and undistorted competition in the European market. Hence the expansion of the European mandate, brought about by the Maastricht Treaty, in the fields of environmental protection and industrial policy, is viewed most critically by authors of this school (Mestmäcker 1992; Behrens 1994). In order to minimize potential damage, it is now also postulated that 'the rights of individuals, granted by the Treaty of the European Communities, to participate in commerce across national borders [must] not be encroached upon by measures in the service of the newly established competencies' (Mestmäcker 1994: 286). If this were accepted, European competition rules would not only constrain national legislation, but would limit 'positive integration' at the European level as well.

[71]

2.3.1 The Need for Agreement

As long as the Luxembourg Compromise of 1966 was applied to all Council decisions, the requirement of unanimity led to extremely cumbersome decision processes that were easily blocked by the veto of even a single member government (Sloot and Verschuren 1990). The Single European Act of 1986 was meant to change this by returning to the rule of qualified-majority voting in the Council at least for harmonization decisions 'which have as their object the establishment and functioning of the internal market' (Art. 100A TEC). As a consequence, the decision process is said to have accelerated, since it is now no longer necessary to bargain for every last vote (Dehousse and Weiler 1990; Engel and Borrmann 1991; Hayes-Renshaw and Wallace 1997; but see Golub 1997a). However, voting strengths and voting rules in the Council are still adjusted in such a way that groups of countries united by common interests can rarely be outvoted (Hosli 1996).[31] In any case, the veto still remains available as a last resort even to individual countries when their 'very important interests' are at stake, and the unanimity rule still continues to apply to a wide range of Council decisions. Thus, the need for consensus remains high for measures of positive integration.

Nevertheless, the Community is actively harmonizing national regulation in such areas as health and industrial safety, environmental risks, and consumer protection (Joerges 1994b; Joerges and Neyer 1997; Majone 1993), and it had in fact begun to do so long before the Single European Act

---

[31] Nevertheless, there have been qualified-majority decisions in important cases (Engel and Borrmann 1991). In any case, countries interested in stronger, rather than weaker, legislation are often defeated in the Council—as was true of Denmark, Germany, and the Netherlands with regard to the packaging-waste directive (Golub 1996c).

allowed for qualified-majority voting (Rehbinder and Stewart 1984). It is also reported that these regulations are indeed defining high levels of protection in many areas (Eichener 1992; 1993; 1997; Héritier et al. 1996; Pollack 1997*a*; but see Golub 1996*b*; 1996*d*). How can these findings be reconciled with my claim that positive integration is impeded by the high consensus requirements in the Council of Ministers?

2.3.2 An Intergovernmental Perspective

In searching for an explanation, I will assume that the European Parliament is generally in favour of positive integration, and is using its limited but by no means negligible power (Tsebelis 1994) to extend it through market-correcting European regulations that would offer high levels of protection. I further assume that the same tends to be true of the presidency of the Commission and of the directorates general that are in charge of substantive policy areas other than competition policy (i.e. DG IV). These are, of course, simplifying assumptions that ignore the fact that the creation of the common market, as distinguished from market-correcting interventions, will also rank high among the policy interests of the Parliament and the Commission as a whole. Nevertheless, once the market is established, they are less likely than DG IV to oppose re-regulation *on the European level* on the grounds that the freedom of the market should be protected against any kind of political intervention, national or European, by the 'economic constitution' of the Treaty (Mestmäcker 1994). The assumption is, therefore, that the policy initiatives proposed by the Commission will tend to have a pro-intervention bias that is likely to be supported by the Parliament as well (Pollack 1997*a*). For the sake of argument, I will also assume that the Commission and the Parliament, as well as

[73]

COREPER and other committees preparing decisions of the Council of Ministers, will use the influence they have on the processes of decision in order to facilitate the adoption of Commission proposals in the Council. The implication then is that systematic, as distinguished from contingent, failures of positive integration must find their explanation in the constellation of interests among governments in the Council of Ministers.[32]

In the Council of Ministers, unanimity or qualified-majority voting rules institutionalize veto positions, and it is analytically true that the probability of policy initiatives being blocked increases exponentially with the number of veto positions (Tsebelis 1995). It is equally true, however, that blockages can be overcome through negotiations, and the 'Coase Theorem' tells us that, in principle at least, negotiations will allow the participating parties to realize all outcomes that are Pareto-superior to the status quo (Coase 1960). In other words, Europe is capable of positive action if, and only if, there is a possibility of *common* gains. That is not meant to suggest that European action presupposes a complete convergence of interests (i.e. constellations that could be represented as 'pure coordination games'). The professionalism and dedication of negotiators in COREPER and in the multi-

---

[32] I will thus limit myself here to the simplest form of 'intergovernmental' explanation. It is of course true, as has been pointed out by several critics, that actual interaction patterns are much more complex. In addition to the Commission, the Parliament, and the intensively Europeanized members of COREPER (Hayes-Renshaw and Wallace 1997: ch. 3; Lewis 1997), they include European and national interest organizations (Mazey and Richardson 1993) and individual firms operating at the European level (Coen 1997) as well as subnational governments (Marks 1993; Marks et al. 1996). For present purposes, however, I assume that none of these actors would be willing or able to block market-correcting measures of positive integration if member governments in the Council were willing to adopt them.

tude of committees in which European solutions are being worked out (Pedler and Schaefer 1996; Hayes-Renshaw and Wallace 1997; Joerges and Neyer 1997), and the use of side payments and package deals, would generally allow productive compromises to be reached even when interests are only partly overlapping (i.e. in constellations that could be represented as 'mixed-motive games'—Scharpf 1992; 1997a).

In addition, there is the role of the Commission as 'agenda setter' that must formulate the initiatives on which the Council is able to act. In theoretical analyses, this function is generally considered powerful under conditions of majority voting, where the agenda setter is able to select its most preferred solution among a range of options that could find support among majorities composed of different members (Shepsle and Weingast 1987; Pollack 1997a). But that does not imply that the Commission's monopoly of legislative initiatives should be unimportant if decisions are taken unanimously. Given the heterogeneous conditions represented by member state governments, and their difficulties in arriving at true perceptions of each other's preferences, it may be extremely difficult for them to come to an agreement in multilateral negotiations even if mutually acceptable solutions do exist. By contrast, transaction costs are much lower if the search for an acceptable solution is conducted by a central agent in bilateral negotiations; and if this solution is then proposed by the agenda setter, it will be rational for all governments to vote for it, if that outcome is more attractive to them than the non-agreement outcome (Scharpf 1997a). It seems reasonable, therefore, to think that, by and large, European decision processes are capable of reaching agreed-upon outcomes if solutions do in fact exist that are preferred by all member governments over the status quo. And even if that is not the case, side payments and package deals may allow countries that stand to gain a lot from a European solution to compensate other countries that are willing to sacrifice their weak preference for the status quo if the price is right. In short, empirical examples of successful European policy-making are in no way to be considered theoretical anomalies even from an intergovernmentalist point of view (Eichener 1992; 1997; Héritier et al. 1996; Pollack 1997*b*).[33]

But even if we should assume that, regardless of high transaction costs, all opportunities for mutual gain are in fact exploited and all potential win–win solutions realized, European policy processes will often encounter constellations where no solution is available that would be preferred over the status quo by all, or most, member governments. In such constellations of conflicting interests, in which only win–lose solutions are possible, hierarchical or majoritarian decision systems will still be capable of effective policy-making, whereas negotiation systems and systems depending on qualified majorities requiring high levels of consensus will then be blocked (Scharpf 1988; 1997*a*).[34]

---

[33] Some of the literature cited here takes issue with my analysis of the 'joint decision trap' (Scharpf 1988). In that article, it is true, I have emphasized the importance of transaction costs as an obstacle to unanimous agreement, and I have not sufficiently considered the role of the Commission as agenda setter and of 'comitology' in reducing transaction costs and facilitating agreement. To that extent, my present conclusions would be more optimistic with regard to the European capacity for consensual policy-making. With regard to constitutional changes, however (which after all were the main focus of my 1988 article), I see no theoretical reason for modifying my analysis, and I also see little evidence that would challenge its empirical validity.

[34] Such constellations tend to be underexamined in studies aiming at a general representation of decision structures and practices without regard to specific policy issues—as is true of the masterly work of Fiona Hayes-Renshaw and Helen Wallace (1997). They rightly emphasize, and explain, the fact that agreement is reached in a large portion of cases. By contrast, studies focusing on narrower policy issues have a better chance of observing the difference between original aspirations and the outcomes actually achieved—which in some areas can be very large (Golub 1996*c*; Streeck

2.3.3 Non-Negotiable Intergovernmental Conflicts

If that is so, the problem-solving capacity of the European Community depends on the empirical importance of issues that are characterized by non-negotiable policy conflicts among member governments. What we need to know, therefore, is in which policy areas such conflicts are likely to arise, and how important these areas are likely to be for the overall legitimacy of democratic governance in Europe.

As a first approximation, it seems plausible to distinguish among three types of policy conflicts that are likely to generate blockages of negotiated policy solutions. They involve policies in which one side or the other would either be required to abandon a strong ideological commitment, or would have to sacrifice its fundamental economic self-interest, or would have to incur prohibitive costs of institutional change.

Ideological Conflicts

Non-negotiable conflicts may and do arise from fundamentally opposed normative or ideological positions held by member governments. This is not meant to refer to the ubiquitous policy conflicts generated by the competition among political parties in nation states. In that regard, European negotiations differ from structurally similar negotiations in German federalism (Dehousse 1995; Scharpf 1988; 1995): since there is no common European political sphere, the

1997*b*). Even then, however, empirical case studies have difficulty in dealing with the possibility of 'non-decisions' (Bacharach and Baratz 1970)—issues, that is, that never make it onto the political agenda because everybody knows that they could not be effectively dealt with. This methodological problem, I suggest, can only be dealt with by a systematic combination of substantive problem and policy analyses (to identify what should be done) with an analysis of strategic constellations (to identify what could be done by the actors involved) in a given arena (Scharpf 1997*a*).

[77]

political parties constituting national governments are not competing against each other on the European level, and hence they have nothing to gain from simply preventing the success of their opposite numbers. In fact, cooperation between social-democratic Helmut Schmidt and conservative Giscard d'Estaing was as productive for Europe as was cooperation between socialist François Mitterrand and Christian-democratic Helmut Kohl.

What may matter very much, however, are fundamentally conflicting views regarding the proper role of public policy *vis-à-vis* market forces and regarding the role of European policy *vis-à-vis* the nation state. It is the former type of conflict which has often pitted neoliberal governments in Germany and Britain against the more interventionist indus-trial-policy projects championed by France and by the Commission. Conflicts of the second type between De Gaulle's *Europe des patries* and the more integrationist goals of other member states caused political stagnation in the 1960s and 1970s, and similar disputes with Britain, Denmark, and other countries have limited the range of institutional reforms that could be reached at Maastricht and Amsterdam. Since these conflicts involve fundamental convictions, they are not generally amenable to compromise solutions, except perhaps through opting-out arrangements.

Fundamental Conflicts of Economic Self-Interest

A second type of non-negotiable conflict arises from differences in the levels of economic development. After its southern expansion, the European Community now includes member states with some of the most efficient economies in the world alongside others that are still near the level of threshold economies. Thus, in 1994, GDP per capita ranged from $US8.792 in Portugal to $US28.043 in Denmark

(OECD 1996c)—and roughly the same ratio can be assumed for (average)[35] labour productivity. Thus, if Portuguese firms are to remain competitive in the European internal market, they must not only be able to pay much lower wages than are paid in the most productive countries, but the cost burdens imposed by environmental protection, the welfare state, and other regulations must be correspondingly lower as well.[36] In fact, 'total social expenditure' in 1993 amounted to only 16 per cent of GDP in Portugal, but to 31 per cent in Denmark (OECD 1996b). In other words, Portugal spent only one-sixth of the amount per capita that Denmark was spending on social policy, and the same holds, by and large, for expenditures on environmental protection.

Now, if social-welfare and environmental regulations were harmonized at, say, the Danish level, the international competitiveness of economies with lower productivity would be destroyed. If exchange rates were allowed to fall accordingly, the result would be higher domestic prices and, hence, impoverished consumers. If devaluation were ruled out (e.g. in a monetary union), the result would be deindustrialization and massive job losses—just as they occurred in eastern Germany when the relatively backward GDR economy was subjected to the full range of West German regulations under a single currency. Nor would agreement be easier if the costs of social or environmental regulations were not imposed on enterprises, but financed through higher income or consumption taxes. Since average incomes are much lower, the citizens

---

[35] Naturally, Portugal and similarly situated countries (just like eastern Germany) also have islands of above-average productivity, especially in new plants of multinational corporations.

[36] According to surveys conducted by the Swedish employers' association (SAF), overall costs of a man-hour in industry ranged in 1993 between 33 Swedish kroner in Portugal, 56 kroner in Greece, and 204 kroner in Germany (Kosonen 1994).

of less developed countries could not afford regulations at levels of protection that reflect the aspirations and the willingness to pay of citizens in the rich member states. Thus their governments could not, in good faith and with complete information,[37] agree to common European regulations imposing such costs.

Institutional Conflict

The third obstacle to agreement on common European policies is differences among administrative practices, policy patterns, and institutions. As Adrienne Héritier and her collaborators have shown for European environmental policy, differences among national policy styles and administrative practices are difficult to overcome even though the changes required would primarily affect administrative agencies that are under the direct control of the state (Héritier et al. 1996). The difficulties of harmonization are much greater, however, when there are significant differences in national patterns of policy output, and if changes would significantly affect large numbers of citizens and voters. Thus, even if overall levels of welfare spending as a share of GDP are about the same, countries differ greatly in the way these funds are used.

First, there is the basic difference between the Scandinavian model of service-intensive and the Continental model of transfer-intensive welfare states (Esping-Andersen 1990). Thus, in 1993, Sweden and Denmark were spending 6.4 per cent and 4.4 per cent of GDP, respectively, on services for elderly and disabled people and for families, whereas expen-

---

[37] Even in the absence of side payments, there is, of course, always a possibility that governments may fail to object because they lack expertise (Joerges and Neyer 1997) or because they count on loose implementation practices (Mendrinou 1996).

ditures on the same services amounted to less than 1.2 per cent in the Netherlands and in France, to 0.8 per cent in West Germany, and to less than 0.3 per cent in Italy and Belgium (OECD 1996*b*). These differences find their explanation in the fact that the older Continental welfare states are still influenced by the philosophy of the 'Bismarck model' which, at the end of the nineteenth century, was meant to insure the income risks of the single (male) breadwinner in case of invalidity, sickness, unemployment, and old age, while socially essential services were thought to be provided by mothers, wives, and daughters within the family.

But even if only transfers are considered, the differences are remarkable. Thus, in 1993, Italy was spending 52 per cent of its total welfare budget on old-age pensions, whereas in Ireland pensions took only 22 per cent of the welfare budget. By contrast, health care absorbed 28 per cent of the welfare budget in Ireland, but only 18.5 per cent in Denmark. Ireland and Denmark are similar, however, with regard to their emphasis on family allowances which amounted to more than 10 per cent of total social spending in both countries, but reached only 4.9 per cent in the Netherlands, 3.3 per cent in Italy, and 1.0 per cent in Spain (BMA 1996: 14).

Similar differences exist with regard to financing the welfare state. In 1993, general tax revenues accounted for more than 81 per cent of welfare expenditures in Denmark, but only for 44 per cent in the United Kingdom, 27 per cent in Germany, 22 per cent in the Netherlands, and 19.6 per cent in France. By contrast, Continental welfare states shaped in the tradition of the 'Bismarck model' depend primarily on wage-based contributions from employers and workers. These amounted to more than 72 per cent of the welfare budget in France, more than 65 per cent in Belgium, about 60 per cent in Germany and Italy, about 55 per cent in the

United Kingdom and in the Netherlands, 37 per cent in Ireland, and less than 12 per cent in Denmark (BMA 1996: 13).

Finally, and most importantly, there are fundamental differences in the institutional structures of the welfare state and of industrial relations systems. Health care, for instance, is provided by national health systems and financed from the state budget in Britain and in the Scandinavian countries, whereas on the Continent it is typically provided by private or charitable hospitals and by physicians in private practice, all of whom are paid on a fee-for-service basis by (corporatist) insurance schemes. Similarly, old-age pensions in some countries combine a tax-financed basic pension with varieties of compulsory or voluntary supplemental pension insurance systems, while other countries rely entirely on earnings-based compulsory pension schemes that are, again, organized according to corporatist principles. Moreover, some of these are funded systems while in others current pensions must be paid from current contributions.

Similarly, in industrial relations, there are countries with strong and others with weak unions; some of them organized along party-political or ideological lines, others by industry, and still others by skill groups; some of them with highly centralized and others with decentralized wage bargaining; and some of them highly legalistic, others committed to 'free collective bargaining' (Crouch 1993), and so on.

The existence of ideological, economic, and institutional differences among member states will obviously make agreement on common European regulations extremely difficult, and in many cases impossible. Since positive integration, unlike negative integration, does in fact depend on high levels of agreement among member governments, it follows that certain types of policy problems, for which solutions would be politically feasible within each of the member states, are unlikely to be dealt with effectively at the European level. If, at the same time, national solutions are undercut by negative integration and by the pressures of economic competition, the overall result would be a general loss of problem-solving capacity in the multi-level European polity and, hence, a loss of output-oriented democratic legitimacy. It is important to realize, however, that this tentative conclusion cannot be generalized. Policy areas are likely to differ with regard to both the impact of negative integration and regulatory competition on national solutions and the difficulties of positive integration. Thus it is necessary to explore in some greater detail the conditions affecting national as well as European problem-solving capacity in diverse policy areas. This will be done for a variety of fields in the following chapter.

CHAPTER 3

Regulatory Competition
and Re-Regulation

In discussions about the consequences of economic 'global-ization' and of the completion of the European internal mar-ket, it is often taken for granted that the capacity of national governments to regulate and to tax capital, firms, production processes, and products is being greatly reduced. Whereas neoliberal authors celebrate the liberation of markets from the inefficiencies of political control and rent-seeking inter-ests (Mestmäcker 1987; 1994; Streit and Mussler 1995), writ-ers with an interventionist perspective lament the demise of the democratic civilization of capitalism that was achieved in the aftermath of the 'Great Transformation' (Polanyi 1957) after the Depression and the Second World War (Cerny 1994; Streeck 1995a; 1997a). But however much both sides may disagree about the desirability of its consequences, they all seem to agree on the underlying causal model (Genschel 1998).

Negative integration disables existing national policy solu-tions by prohibiting subsidies to producers, monopolistic and cartellized practices in the provision of goods and services, and all regulations that have the effect of protecting domestic producers from foreign competitors or of restricting in any way the free mobility of goods, services, capital, and labour across national boundaries. As a consequence, national firms

This chapter represents a revised version of my introduction to a special issue of the *Journal of European Public Policy* (Scharpf 1997c).

are exposed to more intense competition from suppliers producing under different national systems of taxation, regulation, and industrial relations—which greatly reduces their opportunities for shifting to consumers the costs of higher taxes and wages or more burdensome regulations. At the same time, national capital owners, firms, and skilled professionals are themselves free to move to locations governed by different regulatory regimes.

The theoretically expected result, then, is a form of economically motivated 'regulatory competition'[1] among nation states and unions which undercuts their capacities to regulate and tax mobile factors of production, and to improve the distributive position of labour through collective bargaining (Sinn 1993; Sinn 1996). Since European re-regulation does depend on high levels of consensus, it tends to be blocked by conflicts of interest among national governments, or may at best reach solutions on the level of the lowest common denominator. Moreover, the institutional preconditions for redistributive collective bargaining do not at present exist at the European level, and it is more than unlikely that they could be created in the foreseeable future (Streeck and Schmitter 1991; Visser and Ebbinghaus 1992; Streeck 1996). As a consequence, it is expected that overall in Europe the political capacity for effective intervention is being reduced below the level that was available in the nation state during the post-war decades.

---

[1] In the literature, the term 'regulatory competition' is used in two different senses. On the one hand, it describes the response of national regulators to the international competition for mobile factors of production and mobile tax bases. This is the sense used here. On the other hand, Adrienne Héritier and her collaborators (1996) use the term to describe the fact that member states of the European Union compete with each other in order to influence the content and form of European regulations with a view to minimizing their own adjustment costs.

Empirically, however, the record seems to be much more mixed than this simple causal model would suggest. At the national level, regulatory competition may or may not be manifest; and where it is, it may sometimes lead to a 'race to the top' rather than to the predicted 'race to the bottom'. Moreover, where national regulation is in fact disallowed by negative integration, or displaced by regulatory competition, European regulations will not always be blocked or tend towards the lowest common denominator, but may in fact achieve high levels of protection. These differences have recently been explored by contributions to a special issue of the *Journal of European Public Policy* (Scharpf 1997*c*). In the present chapter, which draws on these contributions, I will try to show that the overall pattern does reflect systematic differences in the characteristic constellations of interest among member states which have to be confronted in various policy areas. In doing so, I will begin with the conditions under which regulatory competition may, or may not, constrain national governance capacity.

3.1 CONSTRAINTS ON NATIONAL PROBLEM-SOLVING

Economic integration confronts existing (and previously well-functioning) national policy systems with the increasing mobility of financial assets, of goods and services, of firms and locations of production, of certain types of highly skilled labour, and of consumers. As a consequence, national policy instruments that worked well in the past have either become unavailable under the legal constraints of negative integration, or have become less effective or more costly as the 'exit option' has become more easily available to the target

[86]

actors. These constraints have affected national capacities for macro-economic management as well as the capacity to regulate economic processes and products. I will begin with a brief review of macro-economic constraints.

3.1.1 Keynesian Full-Employment Policy

At present, almost all member states of the European Union are suffering from extremely high levels of unemployment which are also straining the financial viability of national welfare states. As I pointed out above, these problems had been kept under control until the early 1970s by Keynesian macro-economic policy which, under the Bretton Woods regime of fixed exchange rates, was able to use the instruments of monetary and fiscal policy to stabilize aggregate demand and to vary the attractiveness of real versus financial investments. In the 'stagflation' period following the oil-price shocks of the 1970s, it became clear that expansionary or restrictive fiscal and monetary policy was no longer able to control the dual challenges of demand-deficient unemployment and cost-push inflation. Nevertheless, a few countries with 'corporatist' institutions, which were also able to use wage policy as an instrument of macro-economic management, could still maintain full employment and price stability at the same time (Scharpf 1991).

During the same period, however, the Bretton Woods regime had been replaced by floating exchange rates, and international capital mobility had increased dramatically to the point where national monetary policy had lost the capacity to set real interest rates below the level defined by the international capital markets (with due adjustments for expected moves of the exchange rate). Rather than stimulating real investment in the domestic economy, any attempt to do so in one country would now produce capital outflows, devaluation, accelerating inflation, and higher effective interest rates (Södersten and Reed 1994). This, at any rate, was the lesson which European policy makers thought they had learned from the debacle of Keynesian reflation attempted in the early 1980s by the first Mitterrand government in France. Conversely, if national interest rates are now increased above the international level to combat inflation, the effect will be counteracted by capital inflows, while a revaluation of the currency will increase imports and reduce export competitiveness. In either case, therefore, the desired policy impact will be weakened by the countervailing effects of capital mobility, whereas the undesired side effects will be stronger than they used to be. As a consequence, central banks have everywhere revoked their commitment to Keynesian full employment policies, and are now primarily concerned with maintaining price stability.

Since monetary policy has been removed from the arsenal of employment-creating instruments, governments that nevertheless attempt to increase employment through aggregate demand reflation[2] must now rely on deficit spending alone. But if fiscal reflation cannot rely on monetary policy for low interest rates, it is not only less effective in economic terms, but also more expensive (Garrett 1996). If continued over the medium term, it must result in unsupportable increases of public indebtedness which, sooner or later, will have to be corrected through massive fiscal retrenchment that may wipe out more jobs than were created before. That, at

---

[2] In macro-economic theory, the effectiveness of demand management was denied by monetarism and, more radically, by the rational-expectations literature of the 1970s. In the meantime, however, mainstream economics seems to have returned to the consensus view that changes in aggregate demand will have a real effect on economic activity and employment at least in the short term (Blanchard 1997; Solow 1997; Taylor 1997).

any rate, has been the experience of several European countries that had opened up their capital markets in the 1980s. Compared to the period before liberalization,[3] the loss of boundary control has in effect deprived nation states of the capacity to assure or regain full employment through the macro–economic management of aggregate demand.

3.1.2 Regulatory Competition

Apart from its effect on the capacity for macro–economic management, economic integration also has important consequences for the national capacity to regulate and tax economic activities. The loss of national boundary control and lower costs of transportation and communication make it easier for investors and producers to avoid burdensome national regulations and taxes, and for consumers to avail themselves of products produced under more attractive regulatory and tax regimes. To the extent that governments depend on keeping capital, firms, and production within the country in order to provide jobs, incomes, and revenue, they must also be concerned about the possibility that their own regulations and taxes may drive capital, firms, and jobs out of the country. Increasing international mobility thus creates conditions in which territorial states are forced to engage in *regulatory competition* against each other in order to attract or retain mobile factors of production. *Ceteris paribus*, pressures to reduce regulatory and tax burdens should thus generate a 'race to the bottom' (Vogel 1995), also described as the 'Delaware effect'—named after the American state that was able to attract

---

[3] That is not meant to imply that the process could be reversed. Since so many other factors have changed as well, one cannot claim that by restoring capital transfer controls (if this were technically feasible) countries could return to the full-employment world of the 1960s.

company headquarters by offering the least demanding standards for incorporation (Cary 1974). In his comparative study of environmental policy, however, David Vogel has also shown that this consequence is not inevitable (Vogel 1995). In his view, regulatory competition may also produce a 'California effect' that will induce states to upgrade their regulatory requirements. There is reason, therefore, to examine the theoretical assumptions underlying the Delaware-versus-California controversy.

Political Imitation

First, it should be acknowledged that some areas of national policy are affected neither by the legal injunctions of negative integration nor by the economic pressures of regulatory competition. Nevertheless, *political* pressures, effectuated through 'voice' rather than through 'exit' mechanisms, may induce countries to imitate foreign models of regulation or deregulation if information about the performance of national systems is spreading through transnational communication. Ideally, one might even expect a form of 'political competition' in which the best solutions would spread—the 'Swedish model' in the 1960s, 'Modell Deutschland' in the 1970s, Japan in the 1980s. In the mid-1990s, the supply of such models has expanded to suit all political tastes: the United States, New Zealand, and the United Kingdom for neoliberal radicals, Denmark for left-of-centre red-green aspirations, the Netherlands and Austria for consensus-oriented grand coalitions. Nevertheless, policy imitation remains a difficult and uncertain process whose outcome depends not primarily on the attractiveness of the foreign models but on the domestic conditions affecting their adoption and implementation—witness the painfully slow deregulation of store closing hours in Germany, or the equally slow move to decriminalize soft drugs in several European countries. Such cases of political, rather than economic, pressures on national regulatory systems will not be considered further here.

Competition on Quality or Competition on Price

But even if economic pressures are important, and if regulatory competition is effective, the outcome need not be a 'race to the bottom'. Just as firms in the market may compete not only on price, but also on the quality of their products or services, so competition among national systems of regulation may also be on quality, rather than on cost. But when should one expect one or the other to dominate? For a theoretically valid answer, it is necessary to examine the underlying constellations of interest among national regulators as they are affected by the market competition between domestic and foreign producers. These constellations are likely to differ significantly for regulations affecting the quality of products on the one hand, and regulations affecting the conditions and costs of production on the other hand (Stewart 1993).

3.1.3 Product Regulations

Regulations of product quality may affect the price of the product as well as its usefulness, safety, or attractiveness in the eyes of the consumer.[4] Hence neoliberal advocates of

---

[4] In the literature on standard-setting, Raymund Werle (1993; 1997) has introduced the important distinction between 'coordinative standards' (which are meant to assure technical compatibility between different products) and 'regulatory standards' (which are meant to prevent negative externalities). The former may be defined by the market or by voluntary agreement among producers and, once established, will be followed voluntarily; the latter may need to be imposed by governments and will depend on enforcement. The present discussion focuses on regulatory standards only.

mutual recognition argue that even in the absence of European harmonization regulatory competition will automatically lead to the selection of the optimal system of national regulations—considering its effect on price and product quality at the same time (Streit 1996*a*; 1996*b*). If that were generally true, however, it is unclear how national regulations could be justified in the first place: if consumer choice were able to select the optimal regulation, it should also select the optimal product in the absence of regulation. Thus, product regulations should have no place at all in a neoliberal world unless they are justified as a remedy for some kind of market failure.[5]

One such condition does exist if valid information about quality differences of certain types of products is difficult to obtain, and when buyers have reason to distrust the information provided by better-informed but self-interested sellers. In that case, the market may not reward superior products, even if their superior quality would be highly attractive to consumers. This type of market failure was theoretically analysed, in a justly famous article by George Akerlof (1970), as the 'market for lemons'. It could be overcome by some form of trustworthy quality control and 'certification' by a third party—a function which might be performed by private associations[6] (assuming that they are allowed to perform it under

---

[5] If that is accepted, the interventionist argument for re-regulation at the European level can be based on the same logic: where national regulation is in fact justified by the existence of market failures, regulatory competition and the rule of mutual recognition would re-create the very same market failure (Sinn 1996).

[6] At the beginning of this century, for example, many educational institutions in the United States were willing to submit to the control of private certification organizations in order to assure students and their parents of the superior quality of the (more expensive) education they were providing (Wiley and Zald 1968).

neoliberal interpretations of competition law) or by public regulation and inspection of product quality.

Now, under specific conditions the 'certification effect' of *national* regulations may also play a role in international regulatory competition. That presupposes, first, that consumers are *informed* of differences between national systems of regulations and, second, that these differences affect the *utility* of the product for (self-interested) consumers—as might be true in the case of regulations assuring high levels of protection against health, safety, or financial risks. When both conditions are fulfilled, stringent national regulations may become a competitive advantage for national firms competing in the international market for quality products—in which case there is indeed no reason to think that regulatory competition should induce competitive deregulation. Instead, the certification effect will put pressure on other governments to upgrade their regulatory systems in order to protect their own industries against foreign competitors whose products are *more attractive because they are more highly regulated.*[7] This mechanism explains some aspects[8] of the 'race to the top' in the case of capital-adequacy regulations in the banking sector (Kapstein 1994; Genschel and Plümper 1997),[9] or in the

---

[7] Producers might also adopt the more attractive foreign standard voluntarily, but would then not benefit from the certification effect of national regulations and controls.

[8] For the upgrading of stock market regulations, just as for the banking accord, the fact that US interlocutors (in this case the Security and Exchange Commission) could plausibly threaten to exclude non-conforming foreign firms from the large and attractive American capital market has also been a very important factor—which, analytically, should not be confused with the certification effect.

[9] As Genschel and Plümper have shown, agreement on the Basle Accord of 1988—which standardized capital adequacy requirements for banks under the supervision of the thirteen central banks that were members of the

upgrading of insider-trading regulations on European stock markets (Lütz 1996). In both of these examples, it is indeed plausible that institutional investors and banks engaged in inter-bank lending should be both well informed of, and highly sensitive to, cross-national differences of regulatory regimes. But these conditions surely cannot be assumed to exist everywhere.

At any rate, however, the certification mechanism could not explain the upgrading of auto emission standards in the United States—in the case, that is, for which the term 'California-effect' was first introduced (Vogel 1995). When California introduced its more stringent auto emission standards in the early 1970s, there were no large-scale automobile producers in the state that could gain a competitive advantage over out-of-state competitors. Moreover, and more importantly, the California standard did increase the price of cars without increasing their utility from the point of view of self-interested consumers. Hence car makers would not gain a competitive advantage by adopting the California standard where it was not required by law, and the diffusion of this standard throughout the United States cannot be explained as a 'race to the top' that was caused by regulatory competition.

The explanation which David Vogel (1995) does in fact provide is institutional, rather than economic: in the 1970s, the US Congress passed a statute that specifically authorized the state of California to adopt emission standards that were more stringent than those provided by uniform national legislation. As a consequence, the free-trade regime of interstate commerce was suspended, and California was allowed to

Bank of International Settlements—is better explained by the domestic problems, and the skilful power play, of the American Federal Reserve. But once it was in place, the Basle standard induced non-member states to upgrade their own levels of banking regulations so as to avoid competitive disadvantages for their own banks in inter-bank lending.

exclude from its home market automobiles that did not conform to its own regulations. If that is assured, and if the California automobile market is large and attractive, firms located in other states need to apply California standards in part of their production, and they may then prefer to see these standards adopted generally, rather than having to produce different cars for different local markets.[10] Moreover, political competition also seems to have played a role in Vogel's explanation: the California example seems to have strengthened the environmental lobby in other states, and it may have assured state legislators that there was no adverse voter reaction to be feared when emission standards were raised. In the end, at any rate, standards were again 'harmonized' by national legislation—but now at the California level.

The institutional factors explaining the California example also exist at the international level when free-trade regimes permit the continuation of certain types of national regulations even though these operate as non-tariff barriers to trade. Thus, Art. XX of the GATT Treaty allows national measures necessary to protect public morals and health or safety of human, plant, or animal life, and similar public-interest values even though these would otherwise fall under the prohibition of quantitative restrictions. The same is also true of Arts. 36 and 100a, IV of the European Community Treaty which, where they are still applicable under the *Cassis* doctrine, allow countries to exclude foreign products that do not conform to their own regulations. If other countries did the same, however, markets would remain fragmented and producers could not exploit potential economies of scale. Such considerations may prevent a small and export-oriented

---

[10] If demand is relatively price inelastic, or if subsidies and tax incentives help to make it so, the auto industry will of course gladly be compelled to sell more expensive cars.

country from raising its own regulatory standards. For a country that controls a relatively large and attractive market, however, the same consideration may be an incentive to impose higher standards—which then may have to be followed by producers in smaller countries in order to avoid competitive disadvantages. Thus, the fact that the United States is the most important market for pharmaceuticals has the effect that many foreign manufacturers will 'voluntarily' comply with American rules for drug testing, rather than incurring large research and development costs for products that they could sell in their home markets, but not in the United States.

To conclude: in the field of product regulations there are two conditions under which one should not expect a race to the bottom. First, foreign products may still be kept out if they do not conform to national regulations serving valid health, safety, or environmental purposes. When that is true, there is no regulatory competition that could exert downward pressures on countries with high levels of regulation. Second, national regulations may serve as a certificate of superior product quality that is rewarded by the market. When that is true, high levels of regulation may even create a competitive advantage for the firms subjected to them, and thus exert a competitive pressure on other governments to raise their own levels of regulation. In short, national product regulations may not be affected by negative integration, and if they are, regulatory competition may, under certain conditions, induce a race to the top, rather than a race to the bottom.

3.1.4 Process Regulations

None of these factors can be counted on to sustain national measures which increase the cost of production without affecting the quality of the product itself. In principle, that is true of environmental regulations of production processes, of social regulations of working conditions, employment security, and industrial relations, and of taxes and levies on capital, labour, and other factors of production. GATT and WTO rules, it is true, allow states to protect themselves against some forms of ecological and social 'dumping', and to use a variety of general and exceptional 'safeguards' to protect threatened industries (Hoekman and Kostecki 1995: chs. 7 and 8). Within the internal market of the European Community, however, none of these exceptions could be used to keep out products that were produced under conditions that do not conform to national process regulations regarding, say, air pollution, work safety, sick pay, codetermination, or minimum wages. Since none of these affect the products themselves, national authorities also cannot count on purely self-interested consumers[11] to prefer goods and services produced under more stringent process regulations. Hence, if process regulations increase the cost of products, regulatory competition will generally exert downward, rather than upward, pressures on national regulations.

But, of course, pressures may be resisted. Thus, the outcome will be determined by the relative strength of the economic pressures that would reduce, and of the political pressures (or the political inertia) that would maintain, the existing level of regulation. This balance of forces will vary from one case to another. Nevertheless, there are characteristic similarities within specific policy areas which may allow

---

[11] When consumers are not self-interested, information about the process of production may also affect sales. Examples that come to mind are the 'union label' on garments in the United States, the 'blue angel' certificate for ecologically superior products in Germany, 'ethical investment' criteria for industrial equities, and the 'Brent Spar' boycott of Shell gasoline. Thus it is indeed possible that some aspects of process regulations may become 'productified'.

some useful generalizations to be formulated. I begin with the empirically most ambivalent area of environmental process regulations.

Environmental Process Regulations

As Vogel (1995; 1997) has shown, existing environmental process regulations seem to be relatively immune to the downward pressures of regulatory competition, even though they neither justify the exclusion of foreign products nor provide tangible benefits to self-interested consumers. As an explanation, Vogel emphasizes the fact that many of these regulations will add only marginally to the costs of production, so that the downward pressure exerted by economic interests will be relatively weak. The same may be true of existing rules protecting health and safety at work (Eichener 1992; 1997). Moreover, the costs imposed by environmental and safety regulations will vary from one sector to another, and the intensity of international competition also varies widely between different sectors. Thus, the economic pressure to reduce existing levels of protection will be strongest in industries exposed to intense international competition, and in areas where regulation adds significantly to the total costs of production. In other industries, these pressures may be much lower.

However, economic costs cannot fully explain political outcomes. An equally or more important factor is the *political* salience of the purposes served by the regulation in question, and the strength of the *political* opposition against their dismantling. Hence, international economic competition will least affect regulations that have the purpose of preventing or abating conditions or activities that are considered harmful in themselves. In that case, economic losses are accepted as a necessary and anticipated consequence, rather than as a misfortune to be avoided. Thus, some environmental regulations may be maintained at the national level even though it is clear that they will conflict with certain economic interests and drive certain types of production out of the country. Taking both factors together, it is indeed plausible that the empirical record should not provide evidence for a *general* race to the bottom in the field of environmental process regulations.

Taxation of Mobile Factors or Persons

The situation is different in the case of taxation. First, the purpose of taxing capital incomes, profits, property, and factors of production is generally revenue collection and, perhaps, redistribution, but not the abatement of certain types of activity. On the contrary, tax policy would become self-defeating if it were to destroy the bases of taxation or to drive them out of the country. This is the argument underlying the famous Laffer curve, and it is clear that the 'revenue-maximizing rate of taxation' is much reduced everywhere if the taxes of one state can be easily avoided by moving the tax base to another state with lower rates. Thus, if the purpose of taxation is revenue maximization, and if the revenue collected depends on the size of the tax base as well as on the tax rate, international competition will create a temptation for states (but in particular for relatively small states) to cut tax rates in the hope that this will increase their tax base sufficiently to increase total revenue. As a result, other states are forced to respond in kind in order to prevent the outflow of taxable resources, and all states will collect less revenue from mobile factors than they would have preferred to do, and could have done, in the absence of transnational mobility and international tax competition (Steinmo 1994; Genschel and Plümper 1997).

If revenue maximization were the only concern, however, the 'race to the bottom' should bottom out before zero tax levels are reached. But when we consider the taxation of real assets, states are not only interested in revenue, but also in the creation or maintenance of jobs. In pursuing this objective in the face of international competition, they may be tempted not only to forgo taxation of real investments altogether, but to subsidize firms and investment capital instead (Gordon and Bovenberg 1996). It is here then, that regulatory competition is likely to take its greatest toll in terms of the national capacity to tax mobile factors. Unfortunately, however, while the compatibility of state subsidies with standards of undistorted competition is now closely scrutinized by the European Commission, no such criteria are as yet applied to competitive *general* reductions of the tax rates applying to capital incomes and businesses.

Social-Policy Regulations

Social policy, finally, shares some of the characteristics that are relevant in the field of taxation, and some that were discussed above with regard to environmental policy. Some social regulations clearly have the purpose of abating certain types of activity—the employment of children, for instance, or various types of hazardous or morally obnoxious work. From the point of view of national policy makers, certain 'bad jobs' simply should not exist, and if they disappear, that should be counted as a social-policy success—even if that success may have an economic price. At the opposite end of the spectrum, financing social security, health care, and other welfare transfers and services through employers' contributions or payroll taxes has all the characteristics just discussed with regard to taxation. Such rules clearly do not have the purpose of destroying jobs, and they become self-defeating if that should be their effect.

For that reason, they are highly vulnerable to the pressures of international regulatory competition.

But most types of social regulations are likely to be located between those extremes. Rules regarding working hours, vacations, working conditions, employment security, sick leave, maternity leave, collective bargaining, and codetermination rights of workers are meant to change the nature of the employment relationship, rather than merely imposing a tax on employers. Their purpose is, in the neo-Marxist jargon, the 'decommodification of labour'. Nevertheless, this goal would be frustrated if 'commodified' jobs simply disappeared, instead of being transformed. For that reason, social-policy regulations that have the effect of, or that are perceived as, reducing profits, and hence capital incomes, are also vulnerable to increased capital mobility. The same is true of codetermination rights which, even if they do not impose monetary costs, are generally perceived as a burden on capital since they reduce managerial discretion in organizing the labour process (Streeck 1997a). Compared to taxation, however, the race to the bottom will at least be impeded by the political commitment of national governments to social-policy purposes and by the political resistance of the groups that would suffer from deregulation and cutbacks (Pierson 1994; 1996).

3.1.5 Constraints on National Problem-Solving

In conclusion, it seems reasonable to expect that the impact of economic integration and of regulatory competition on national problem-solving will vary among policy areas. The capacity for Keynesian full-employment strategies is generally reduced, while the impact on the capacity to regulate and tax economic factors and activities is conditioned by a variety of economic, institutional, and political factors. For product standards, regulatory competition may, under narrowly specified conditions, even create incentives for raising, rather than lowering, existing national levels of protection. Beyond that, international and European free-trade rules allow product-related national health, safety, and environmental regulations to be maintained even though they may have the effect of non-tariff barriers. In the field of taxation, by contrast, increasing transnational mobility will—*ceteris paribus*—reduce the capacity of national governments to tax mobile factors of production and other mobile tax bases. By the same token, environmental and social regulations of production processes are also affected by downward pressures as transnational mobility increases. But here the forces of resistance to environmental and social deregulation and to welfare cutbacks will be stronger, and thus outcomes are likely to be more contingent, than is true in the case of taxation.

Nevertheless, in the field of environmental and social process regulations as well as in taxation, the increasing international competition will generally exert downward pressures on the capacity of national governments to achieve the regulatory purposes that had found political support in past decades. Thus, if these purposes are to be maintained, it would be advantageous if they could be pursued through regulation at the European or international levels.[12] There, however, problem-solving can generally not rely on hierarchical or majoritarian capacities for conflict resolution but depends on agreement among the national governments and

---

[12] I will not here discuss the question of whether European regulations could be economically effective under conditions of world-wide capital mobility and economic globalization. The answer is likely to vary from one policy area to another, and it also depends very much on assumptions about the probability of protectionist policies of the European Union (or of the Monetary Union).

supranational actors involved (and often between these and non-governmental actors as well).

3.2 RE-REGULATION AT THE EUROPEAN OR INTERNATIONAL LEVEL?

Since minority interests cannot be overruled in negotiations at the international level (and must also be largely respected under rules of qualified-majority voting in European policy processes), re-regulation generally has to overcome two problems. The first is the difficulty of reaching agreement among national governments and other veto actors on a common rule, and the second is the problem of assuring faithful implementation once agreement has been reached. Obviously, both of these difficulties depend on the underlying constellation of interests or ideological preferences among the negotiating parties, and hence any attempt to assess the likelihood of success or failure of European or international solutions to the problems that nation states cannot effectively handle any more depends critically on the correct understanding of the underlying constellation.

Clearly, if the constellation is one of pure ('zero-sum') conflict of interest, agreement could not be expected,[13] and if the constellation should resemble a pure coordination game, both agreement and implementation would be unproblematic.[14] Beyond these—analytically—easy cases, however, we

---

[13] Or, rather, any agreement would presuppose the acceptance of common norms of distributive justice.

[14] In determining these characteristics, it is important to keep in mind that what matter are the constellations *among the parties involved in the specific interactions*, rather than constellations among the underlying social or economic interests—which may, or may not, be represented by national governments, the European Commission, or the European Parliament.

are dealing with mixed-motive constellations where seemingly small differences in assumptions about actor preferences can lead to greatly differing hypotheses or predictions. In particular, it is necessary to warn of the tendency, quite widespread among social scientists who are new to using game-theoretical explanations, to interpret all constellations in terms of the symmetrical Prisoner's Dilemma (Scharpf 1997*a*). Such constellations do occur, and they are often highly salient, but they are by no means ubiquitous. Again, therefore, it is useful to consider several policy areas separately.

3.2.1 Market-Making Regulations

One constellation which in fact resembles the symmetrical Prisoner's Dilemma is negotiations among similarly placed states regarding the liberalization of trade and the opening of markets—in other words, negative integration and 'market-making' measures of positive integration. Here it is indeed plausible to think that each country would benefit from gaining access to the larger international market, but would be tempted to continue its own protectionist practices. Under such conditions, agreement may be possible, but even if it is reached, there is a temptation to free-ride at the implementation stage.

As was discussed in the previous chapter, the European Community has solved this problem by enshrining negative integration in the original Treaties, and imposing its current judicial interpretation as part of the *acquis communautaire* on all members that entered the Community thereafter. Moreover, compliance is anything but voluntary: enforcement is a responsibility of the Commission, which can apply decisions and Treaty infringement procedures against national governments, but it may also be achieved by private parties claiming a violation of European competition law in ordinary cases before national courts. Nevertheless, as the 1997 controversy over subsidies to Volkswagen in Saxony illustrated once more, the temptation to violate the rules of negative integration at the implementation stage is alive even after forty years of enforcement of the European Treaties.[15] The same is, of course, even more true for the liberalization of trade through GATT and WTO rules.

Moreover, the assumption that market-integrating policies represent a *symmetrical* Prisoner's Dilemma is not always well founded. Countries and industries are often not similarly placed in relation to the market. Small, open economies have more to gain from liberalization than countries with larger internal markets, and highly efficient industries will benefit at the expense of less efficient, and hitherto protected, competitors. Under such conditions, market liberalization may itself become a highly contentious issue. The difficulties are well illustrated by Adrienne Héritier's (1997) study of the conflict between the Netherlands and Britain on the one hand, and Germany, France, and Italy on the other hand, in European road transport policy. Another example would be the difficult liberalization of European energy markets (S. Schmidt 1997*b*). In these cases, there is no presumption of a common interest in the creation of a larger market. Constellations are more likely to resemble asymmetrical conflict games, and

---

[15] That, at least, was the interpretation of the Commission (and presumably of other member states of the EU). From a German point of view, however, the issue was not (only) free trade versus protectionism, but the defence of a long-standing political (and in fact constitutional) commitment to interregional equalization in the face of much greater economic inequality after German unification. That is why Saxony's prime minister, Kurt Biedenkopf, found it appropriate to challenge the democratic legitimacy of the Commission's intervention—a response that would be incomprehensible if the dispute were simply over competition-distorting subsidies.

agreement may depend on package deals and/or on the threat of hierarchical imposition by the European Court of Justice.

3.2.2 Product Standards

Product standards often have characteristics that are very similar to those of market-making regulations. As discussed above, the rules of negative integration generally leave states free to maintain their own product regulations if these serve valid health, safety, and environmental purposes. Hence, if there is a strong interest in the opening of wider markets, member states must also have an interest in harmonizing product standards. Moreover, since Art. 100 A TEC allows countries to adopt more demanding standards even after harmonization, high-regulation countries are in a relatively strong bargaining position with regard to the level of protection provided by common product rules (Stewart 1993). Agreement is made difficult, however, if existing regulations differ among states, and if the sunk costs of national investments in hardware and procedures have great weight.[16] In game-theoretic terms, such constellations have the characteristics of a 'Battle of the Sexes' game where, if agreement is in fact reached, implementation should not be a problem at all since all parties have an interest in adhering to a common standard once it is observed by others.

It is under such conditions that the agreement-facilitating functions, discussed above, of the Commission's power of agenda-setting, and of 'comitology', have their greatest prac-

---

[16] If disagreement over the preferred solution is strong enough, or if the 'installed base' carries great weight, harmonization may fail altogether—as was true of the attempt, carried on for many years, to define common European standards for electrical plugs and sockets.

tical importance. Accordingly, there is now a considerable literature, based on a wide range of empirical studies, showing that agreement on common European product standards offering high levels of protection has in fact been reached in a variety of fields including foodstuff regulations (Joerges and Neyer 1997), consumer safety, work safety, and environmental regulations affecting marketable products (Eichener 1997; Pollack 1997*b*). The same seems to be true in the service sector with regard to banking and stock market regulations (Lütz 1996; Genschel and Plümper 1997). There are, in other words, important policy areas where problem-solving at the European level may be quite as effective as it is in the more interventionist member states. But, *nota bene*, this is true for product standards precisely because here national problem-solving capacity has not been destroyed by negative integration—and hence, is also less constrained by the economic pressures of regulatory competition.

3.2.3 Work Safety and Environmental Process Regulations

Turning from product to process regulations, it seems useful to begin by drawing a few distinctions. The most important one is between problems which, for technical or legal reasons, can only be dealt with through international cooperation or supranational regulation, and problems of a local nature for which local solutions are legally and technically possible, but may be affected by the economic pressures of regulatory competition.

Global and Border-Crossing Pollution

Problems caused by global or border-crossing pollution or by the exhaustion of global resources can only be dealt with through cooperation or regulation at a level above the nation state. The underlying constellation among nation states is often modelled as a 'Tragedy of the Commons' (Hardin 1968), i.e. as a symmetrical, n-Person Prisoner's Dilemma. That model may indeed be appropriate for such issues as 'global warming', the 'ozone hole', the protection of biological diversity, or the protection of the Antarctic. Even there, however, agreement is made more difficult by important asymmetries with regard to the benefits expected from regulation, and even more so with regard to the distribution of the costs of abatement, and the ability to bear these costs (Mitchell 1994; Oye and Maxwell 1994). In spite of such asymmetries, however, the constellation still retains important characteristics of the Prisoner's Dilemma in so far as all parties have a common interest in avoiding the destruction of common resources (Keohane and Ostrom 1994). Under such conditions, negotiated agreement is not impossible, but it may critically depend on side payments that will induce the cooperation of countries that otherwise would have to bear higher costs or receive lesser benefits from cooperation. This seems to be characteristic of recent global regimes protecting the biosphere (Ward 1993; Zürn 1995). Even then, however, agreements are likely to encounter free-rider problems at the implementation stage.

Negotiated agreement will be still more difficult to reach in the case of border-crossing water and air pollution, such as when acid rain is being transported from England to Sweden or chemical waste from Switzerland to Germany and the Netherlands. Such issues should be represented by asymmetric conflict games, rather than by the Prisoner's Dilemma. If they are considered in isolation, a purely self-interested upstream polluter country will have no interest in abatement, and could only be bribed to cooperation through offers of side payments or package deals—or through threats of retaliation in other policy areas. Moreover, even if agreement is reached,

[108]

implementation and the monitoring of compliance are likely to remain serious issues.

Local Problems Affected by Regulatory Competition

The second type of constellation concerns pollution and work-safety problems of a local or regional scope which, under technical aspects, would not require international action. Nevertheless, as shown by Eichener (1992; 1997), Héritier and collaborators (1996), or by Pollack (1997*b*), there is in fact a considerable body of European work-safety and environmental regulations that are dealing with production processes, rather than product quality, and that are not addressed to border-crossing pollution problems. The motive for such regulations follows from the consequences of *economic* integration discussed above: governments, unions, and environmental groups that find themselves constrained at the national level by the downward economic pressures of regulatory competition will be attracted by the promise of re-regulation at a level from which the larger European market could be subjected to uniform rules. Moreover, business interests in high-regulation countries may also be attracted by the prospect of a more 'level playing field' that reduces their competitive disadvantage.[17]

[17] More doubtful may now be the *legal* competence of the Union to adopt environmental process regulations. Under the 'subsidiarity' clause introduced by the Maastricht Treaty into Art. 3b TEC, the claim that the objectives of process regulations 'cannot be sufficiently achieved by the member states' is easily justified only for the regulation of border-crossing pollution, but difficult to substantiate for regulations whose purpose is to prevent distortions of competition that could result from differences among national regulations dealing with local pollution problems. In other words, a desire for 'level playing fields' can no longer automatically justify European initiatives, and the Commission seems to have already responded to anticipated objections by Britain and other member states (Golub 1996*b*).

In some areas, moreover, European action is facilitated by factors that are similar to those affecting product regulations. Work safety and emission control at the workplace are often incorporated in the machinery of production itself, so that a larger European market for modern machine tools may in fact depend on the creation of common European standards. Moreover, the electronic revolution in production technologies is accelerating the obsolescence of existing national standards, and the most mobile firms which are likely to work with the most modern production tools would lose internal economies of scale if they were to employ obsolete machinery in low-regulation locations. It is quite likely therefore that influential industrial associations and multinational firms will support, rather than oppose, Europe-wide health, safety, and environmental standards for machine tools and office equipment even if these should be formulated above the level of presently existing national regulations.

But that is not generally true in the field of environmental process regulations. Assuming that stringent regulations do in fact impose burdens on firms which these would prefer to avoid, regulatory competition creates a Prisoner's Dilemma constellation for national governments. By itself, it is true, this would not preclude European solutions since the symmetrical Prisoner's Dilemma should be easily resolved when enforceable agreements are possible. Thus the fact that it is possible to find examples of effective environmental process regulations at the European level should not come as a theoretical surprise. Unfortunately, however, these examples cannot be generalized (Golub 1996*d*)—and that also should not come as a theoretical surprise. The benign implications are derived from the assumption of a *symmetrical* Prisoner's Dilemma which, in the environmental field, would imply that all governments should be similarly concerned about problems of environmental pollution, and similarly affected by the

[110]

pressures of economic competition and by the economic consequences of proposed regulations. Among the member states of the European Union, these conditions will often not be fulfilled.

Even countries with objectively similar levels of pollution and in similar economic conditions may differ significantly with regard to the 'environmental consciousness' of public opinion or with regard to the political influence of 'green' parties and pressure groups. Even more important are objective differences among member states in the intensity of pollution problems and in levels of economic development, and hence in industrial productivity. Thus measures of environmental protection that correspond to the willingness and ability to pay of citizens and firms in highly developed countries may be perceived as being prohibitively expensive in the less productive economies. When that is true, the constellation again assumes the characteristics of an asymmetrical conflict game (Scharpf 1996). On theoretical grounds, one should then expect that uniform regulations at the level of protection demanded by, say, Denmark, the Netherlands, and Germany are likely to fail at the European level (Golub 1996*c*). If they are accepted nevertheless, side payments to 'cohesion countries' may have had to play a large role, and even then the agreement on common rules may not assure uniform implementation.

However, the relative weights of these factors are likely to vary greatly from one case to another, and it is therefore to be expected that the empirical record will be characterized by high variance. It is also to be expected that the interests pulling in either direction will often be nearly in balance, and that therefore specific institutional conditions, and contingent strategies pursued by the Commission or by a member government, may shift the balance toward success or failure.

[111]

3.2.4 Social Regulations

In principle, what has just been said applies also to the international harmonization of social regulations. Again, agreement would be relatively easy to achieve if all countries had an interest in avoiding the 'race to the bottom' and if there were no important asymmetries in their interest constellations. But again, ideological preferences differ between governments committed to high levels of welfare-state protection, and governments emphasizing reliance on the self-help of individuals and families. Moreover, differences in the level of economic development also imply widely differing abilities to pay for welfare-state transfers and services, or to absorb the costs of social regulations. But that is not all. As I pointed out at the end of the last chapter, even among the more highly developed welfare states structural differences of welfare spending are so important that agreement on uniform rules would be met by strong political resistance from those groups whose benefits would be reduced through harmonization. Even more important are institutional differences among European welfare states that are based on different sources of finance, have developed different principles of organization, and make use of different mixes of transfers and social services and of public, not-for-profit and private service provision (Esping-Andersen 1990). To move from there to a uniform European system of social protection would require revolutionary changes in those countries that would have to switch to a different type of institutional regime—say from a tax-financed and publicly provided national health care system to a health insurance system paying for privately provided health services, or from a pay-as-you-go social-security system to a funded pension insurance. The same is generally true in the field of industrial relations (Visser and Ebbinghaus 1992; Crouch 1993). In all of these areas, institutional and structural differences even among countries that are committed to high levels of social protection would create enormous obstacles to the harmonization of social and industrial-relations policy by international agreement (Streeck 1995*a*; 1997*b*).

3.2.5 Taxation

Some of the same difficulties will also stand in the way of harmonizing capital and business taxes. In addition, tax harmonization would have to cope with specific difficulties arising from differences in the size of countries. If tax competition is driven by the hope that lower tax rates will be over-compensated by an enlargement of the tax base, the effect must be particularly attractive for small countries whose tax revenues will benefit disproportionately from an inflow of capital from larger countries. The initial tax loss is further minimized, if rates are reduced only for foreign firms—with the consequence that large industrial firms are now setting up special financing corporations to finance all their investments from (and accumulate all their profits in) countries with particularly low corporation taxes. Given these temptations, it seems less surprising that all initiatives to harmonize corporation taxes within the EU have failed over many years than that the economic and finance ministers did at least agree on a political 'code of conduct' for the taxation of foreign corporations in December 1997. For similar reasons, several attempts to harmonize withholding taxes on interest income have foundered on the opposition of Luxembourg and of the United Kingdom—the former defending its status as a tax shelter for German money, and the latter concerned about the position of the London city in competition with New York and Tokyo (Genschel and Plümper 1997). Analytically, the conclusion seems clear therefore: in the field of European tax harmonization, national governments are probably motivated by divergent definitions of fiscal and economic self-interest. However, even if all were single-minded revenue maximizers, it is not true that tax competition would be equally damaging, or tax harmonization equally beneficial, for all member governments. This heterogeneity of interests has so far frustrated attempts to harmonize taxes on business and capital incomes. As a consequence, tax competition continues to drive down the share of total government revenue that is generated by taxes on business and capital incomes (OECD 1997*b*)—and it has forced governments to shift ever larger shares of total revenues to taxes on immobile factors, in particular to taxes on wages and on consumption (*The Economist* 1997).[18] Hence, in addition to increasingly tighter constraints on the overall capacity to raise revenue, these changes are undermining the perceived justice (and hence the legitimacy) of the tax system.

3.2.6 Macro-economic Management

Among policy makers of a Keynesian persuasion, there is still a hope that the capacity for macro-economic full-employment strategies that was lost at the national level might be recovered at the European level, either through the policy choices of European institutions or through coordinated action among the member governments of the Union. This, surely, must be the hope behind the employment art-

[18] This conclusion is disputed by Swank (1997) and Garrett (1998). However, Swank did include payroll taxes in his definition of taxes on capital (rather than treating them as a tax on labour as a relatively immobile production factor), whereas Garrett is using data that include taxes on the most immobile tax base, landed property, among taxes on capital.

icles adopted at Amsterdam on the insistence of the incoming socialist government in France. The past record, however, is not encouraging.

With regard to monetary policy, whatever policy coordination there was in fact, was achieved by the commitment of national banks to stabilize the exchange rate of national currencies against the Deutschmark. This had the effect of spreading the impact of the Bundesbank's tight-money policy throughout Europe which, if it did not destroy jobs, certainly did not help to create additional employment. In fact, during the 1990s, economic activity was most stimulated in those European countries whose currencies were bounced from the European Monetary System by currency speculation. Since, under the terms of the Maastricht Treaty, the future European Central Bank is supposed to be even more independent than, and as committed to price stability as, the Bundesbank, it is hard to see how European monetary policy could do much more for employment in the future.[19]

In order to achieve any employment effect at all against a tight-money policy of the central bank, fiscal impulses would have to be very large indeed—much larger, at any rate, than what could be achieved within the comparatively minute budget of the European Union. Coordinated national expansion would be a different matter, but here the coordination

[19] To repeat, I am not claiming that Keynesian macro-economic concertation at the European level could bring about full employment in Europe. What matters is that the institutional arrangements adopted at Maastricht and Amsterdam are designed to rule out even the attempt to do so. There is, however, one difference that might justify a slightly more optimistic prediction: the EMU area will have a much smaller external contribution than Germany. Thus, the Bundesbank could often count on export-led growth to compensate for a weakness of domestic demand, whereas the European Central Bank will have to take domestic demand more seriously.

that was in fact achieved by the deficit criteria of the Maastricht Treaty has forced all countries aspiring to membership in the European Monetary Union to adopt deflationary, rather than expansionary fiscal strategies. Moreover, if the Monetary Union should come about, the 'stability pact' signed at Amsterdam represents a commitment to extend fiscal discipline into the indefinite future. In short, European integration has so far not helped to overcome the constraints imposed on Keynesian full-employment policies at the national level, and the rules adopted for the European Monetary Union are not designed to change that situation.

3.3 CONCLUSION

The main message of this chapter is addressed to theory-oriented students of public policy in Europe: there is no reason to expect that *general* propositions will explain and predict either the impact of economic integration on the national governance capacities, or the capacity of European or international institutions to deal effectively with problems in those areas where national solutions are in fact undermined. Thus, the fact that existing empirical studies come to widely differing conclusions, some highly optimistic, others deeply pessimistic, need not imply that at least some of these authors must be wrong. Instead, it is quite likely that the cases studied are dealing with different constellations in which different outcomes should be expected. Thus, if research should not merely provide descriptions of the empirical variance, but aim at theory-based explanations and predictions, it will be necessary to identify those differentiating factors and causal mechanisms that affect the outcome one way or another.

My attempt to do so has drawn separate attention to the factors permitting or reducing national regulatory capacities, and the factors facilitating or constraining regulation at the European level. At the national level, regulatory capacity is constrained, first, by the legal prohibitions of 'negative integration' which rule out measures that could restrain trade or distort competition. But even where national regulations are legally permissible, a second, economic, constraint is defined by the downward pressure of regulatory competition. Its intensity varies from one field to another, and the same is true of the strength of the political forces defending existing levels of national regulation and social protection. Thus, the horizontal axis in Fig. 3.1 represents a composite measure of these

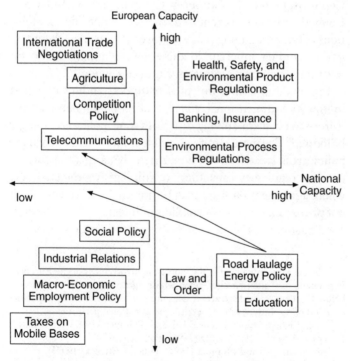

Fig. 3.1. National and European problem-solving capacities

[117]

legal, economic, and political factors defining the remaining national capacity to regulate.

The vertical axis representing the capacity for European action is again defined by collapsing two sets of factors. In the legal dimension, the Union is able to exercise certain exclusive competencies, while in other areas its jurisdiction is tightly constrained or non-existent. In the political dimension, European capacity is constrained by the need for unanimous, or nearly unanimous, agreement among member state governments in the Council of Ministers. This need is reduced or eliminated in areas where the enforcement of negative integration (and the definition of its scope) is left to the Commission and the European Court of Justice. But where Council agreement is required, the policy-specific constellations of interest among national governments, and the intensity of conflict inherent in these constellations, define the most important constraints on European action.[20]

Fig. 3.1 represents my present understanding of where in this two-dimensional conceptualization of national and European problem-solving capacities some policy areas might be located. The more 'optimistic' case studies[21] tend to focus on policy areas located in the upper right-hand quadrant where national regulatory capacities are still legally protected, and where agreement on European (or international) standards is not prevented by massive conflicts of interest. The lower left-hand quadrant is the focus of the 'pessimistic' case studies.[22] It

[20] In this conceptualization the increasing involvement of the European Parliament just adds another actor whose agreement must be obtained before the Union is able to act. It does not provide majoritarian capacities for conflict resolution, as is generally true of national parliaments.

[21] e.g. Eichener (1997); Genschel and Plümper (1997) on banking; Joerges and Neyer (1997); Lütz (1996); Pollack (1997b).

[22] e.g. Genschel and Plümper (1997) on taxes; Streeck (1997b).

represents the location of policy areas where national capacities are economically constrained by the severe downward pressure of regulatory competition while European action remains blocked by severe conflicts of interest among national governments or, in the case of macro-economic employment policy, by institutional arrangements designed to rule out a range of policy options at both the national and the European level.

The remaining two quadrants represent the location of policy areas that have either been successfully Europeanized or that remain under national control. But the latter also include policy areas in which national control is currently being lost. The arrows in the diagram represent the possibility that control might be shifting to the European level—which was true in telecommunications, where economic competition had weakened the effectiveness of national regulations and where the European Commission was then able to liberalize the sector. Member states have also lost most of their capacity to regulate road haulage (Héritier 1997), and the same is about to happen in the market for electricity (S. Schmidt 1997*b*). But whereas in telecommunications the Commission is also ready to provide the degree of re-regulation that seems to be required, it is as yet unclear whether that will be possible in the transport and energy fields. It may still turn out that the Commission and the Court did succeed in disempowering national regulatory capabilities, while severe conflicts of interest will prevent the development of adequate European capabilities.

The overall picture is, therefore, extremely varied and does not justify any generalized conclusions about gains and losses in political problem-solving capacity that have been caused by world-wide economic and European economic and political integration. But there are indeed areas where such losses

[119]

should be expected on theoretical grounds. In Fig. 3.1, this would be true of policy areas located in the lower left-hand quadrant of the diagram. It is on these policy areas that the following chapters will concentrate.

CHAPTER 4

National Solutions without Boundary Control

There are, then, indeed policy areas where the legal force of negative integration and the economic pressures of transnational factor mobility and regulatory competition have significantly reduced the problem-solving capacity of national political systems, and where this loss is not compensated by corresponding gains in European problem-solving capacity. Unfortunately, these include areas that are close to the core of output-oriented democratic legitimacy as it has evolved during the post-war decades in European welfare states (Marshall 1975). At the very minimum, their citizens have come to expect that the democratic state should be able

- to prevent mass unemployment that would exclude large parts of the working-age population from active participation in the processes of social production;
- to prevent extreme poverty that would force persons to live below socially acceptable levels of income and access to life chances; and
- to assure a fair sharing of benefits and tax burdens.

The glaring failure to maintain even these minimal assurances during the Great Depression destroyed the legitimacy of democratic government in Weimar Germany, and put it at risk in other countries. At any rate, in trying to cope with threatening legitimacy crises, most democratic governments found themselves forced to resort to protectionist policies that destroyed the integrated world economy of the time (Röpke 1942). After the Second World War, therefore, world markets were only gradually reintegrated under American-led international regimes that have been aptly characterized as 'embedded liberalism' (Ruggie 1982). They were in fact able to strengthen democratic legitimacy because they allowed national welfare states to gain economic benefits from international integration while maintaining or increasing the protection of their citizens against the 'creative destruction' associated with vigorous capitalism (Gilpin 1987; Eichengreen 1996). In most member states of the European Union, citizens have come to consider these achievements of post-war welfare states as constitutive elements of a legitimizing social contract (Jacquemin and Wright 1993). If they should now be revoked under the pressures of economic globalization or the asymmetry of negative and positive integration in the European Community, there is indeed a danger that rising political disaffection will again undermine either the political legitimacy of democratic governments or their political commitment to economic integration (Ruggie 1994; Leibfried and Rieger 1997). It may not be by accident, therefore, that the radical right-wing opposition in several European countries in also radically anti-European.

There is reason, therefore, to search for options that could restore the political capacity for dealing with mass unemployment, the crisis of the welfare state, and rising inequality at all levels of the multi-level European polity. In the present chapter, I will explore options that even in an internationalized economy could still be pursued nationally. I will begin with employment, and I will try to show how the persistent employment gap in Europe is related to the structures of European welfare states, and in particular to the prevailing mode of financing the welfare state—with the implication that appropriate structural changes could ease both the problems of underemployment and the fiscal crisis of the welfare state. At the end of the chapter, I will then discuss some of the options that might allow national governments to deal with the erosion of their tax base.

4.1 THE EUROPEAN EMPLOYMENT GAP

Present political discussion in Europe emphasizes the superior employment performance of the United States where the rate of unemployment is now lower than it is, on average, in Europe, and where the rate of job creation has been much higher over the last two decades or so. In fact, between 1971 and 1994, civilian employment increased by 55 per cent in the United States, and only by 11 per cent in the present member states of the European Union (OECD 1997c). However, if anything is to be done about this European employment gap, it is first necessary to understand its causes.

In searching for an explanation, Keynesian economists and politicians tend to emphasize contingent factors. For the present decade, it can indeed be argued on good theoretical grounds that macro-economic policy has played an important role in bringing about very high levels of unemployment: even if one should accept the monetarist claim that *expansionary* fiscal and monetary policy, when anticipated, will produce more inflation, rather than more employment, that proposition could not be reversed. Given that wages, and hence prices, are downward-sticky, *restrictive* fiscal and monetary policy is surely able to reduce effective demand and destroy jobs. Hence the tight-money response of the Bundesbank to German unification in the early 1990s must be as much part of the dismal European employment performance as is at present the desperate attempt of practically all European governments to cut budget deficits in order to meet the EMU criteria. These matters are well known, and nothing of interest could be added here.

What is more worrying, however, is the structural component of the European employment gap. It is reflected in the high level of long-term unemployment. In 1995, for instance, only 9.7 per cent of the unemployed in the United States had been out of work for twelve months or longer. Among the member states of the European Union, this ratio varied between 17 per cent in Austria and more than 60 per cent in Belgium and Italy, with most countries having shares of long-term unemployment between 30 and 50 per cent (OECD 1996a: table Q). As everywhere, the main victims of long-term unemployment are unskilled workers and young job seekers with low levels of schooling.

For an explanation of the structural component of the European employment gap, most commentators see little need to search beyond the usual suspects that were blacklisted in the notorious OECD Jobs Study (1994)—institutional rigidities, union power, and the burdens of the welfare state. In an age of intensified global competition, so it is argued, government regulations and collective-bargaining agreements can no longer be considered 'beneficial constraints' but have become fetters that prevent European firms from achieving the flexibility and innovativeness that allow American firms to compete successfully. In addition, the European economies are labouring under the dead weight of bloated public sectors that are claiming more than 50 per cent of GDP in Sweden and Denmark, more than 40 per cent in France, Germany, and other Continental countries, as compared to less than 30 per cent in the United States and Japan—and of overextended welfare states with overly generous rates of income replacement that have raised reservation wages and reduced the incentives to work.

4.1.1 The Measure of Success: Employment Ratios

In my view, these conventional explanations are not focusing on the critical structural factors. If the employment performance of different countries is to be evaluated and explained, there is, first, a need for valid indicators of success or failure. For this, the usual reference to unemployment figures will not do. They do not include persons on disability pensions, in early retirement, and other forms of paid non-work,[1] and they are notoriously subject to political manipulation—the British Conservatives are said to have changed unemployment definitions more then thirty times during their period in office, each time reducing the number of the registered unemployed. Moreover, and even more importantly, the rate of unemployment is defined by reference to the size of the 'active population' which is, of course, strongly affected by factors on the supply side of the labour market. Thus, the willingness of married women to enter the labour market as job seekers may be as much affected by the separate or joint taxation of spouses' incomes or the availability of day care as it is by the availability of jobs.

Compared to unemployment rates, employment figures and their changes over time seem to be a much better indicator of comparative performance—but they also are affected by changes on the supply side: larger populations imply more jobs. Even when employment figures are normalized by reference to the population of working age (15 to 64), comparability suffers from differences in working time and in the share of part-time employment (which happens to be unusually

---

[1] For a careful comparison of the Dutch and German systems of paid non-work, of which only some forms are counted as 'unemployment', see G. Schmid (1996).

high in the Netherlands, for instance). With this caveat in mind, however, employment/population ratios still seem to be the most valid indicators of relative employment performance for which internationally comparative data are readily available in OECD publications (OECD 1996a; 1997c). I will use them throughout.[2]

Similarly, the causal relationship hypothesized by conventional explanations is not fully captured by the usual reference to the share of taxes and social-security contributions in GDP, since a large (but variable) part of public budgets is actually spent on subsidies to business and on public infrastructure and services that should increase the productivity, and hence the international competitiveness, of national economies.[3] Instead, I will use OECD data on the share of total social expenditures in GDP (OECD 1996b) which, better than other internationally comparable indicators, should indeed reflect the 'dead weight' of the welfare state on the economy that is presumed to explain the poor European employment performance.

Taking the latest available OECD (1997c) data on employment ratios for 1996, and on total social expenditures for 1993 (OECD 1996b), Fig. 4.1 shows that welfare spending as such does not explain the differences in employment ratios. It is true that the United States and some other countries with

[2] It would be possible to use total hours worked as an indicator that neutralizes differences in part-time employment. However, if the underlying normative criterion is the involuntary exclusion of large segments of the population from participation in the process of social production, there is little reason to consider (voluntary) part-time employment as being inferior.

[3] I ignore here the proposition that the welfare state itself should be considered a productivity-increasing factor—either because it allows firms to externalize the social costs of efficiency-increasing decisions, or because it legitimizes free-trade policies pursued by democratic governments (Leibfried and Rieger 1997).

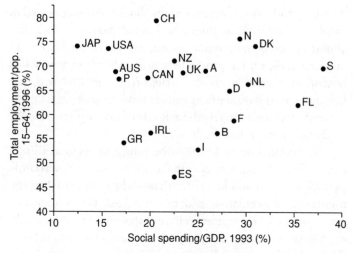

Fig. 4.1. Total employment and social spending

very low shares of social spending had high employment ratios, and it is also true that employment ratios in the more advanced Continental welfare states were significantly lower. At the same time, however, the Scandinavian welfare states with extremely high shares of social spending were also highly successful in employment terms, in some cases reaching levels of employment that were as high as or even slightly higher than in the United States. Overall, in any case, the statistical association between employment and social spending is practically zero. So much for conventional wisdom?

4.1.2 Exposed and Sheltered Sectors

But how could one account for the fact that the most expensive welfare states with the highest tax burden among OECD

[127]

countries and with powerful unions should be doing as well in employment terms as does the United States—which has almost ceased being a welfare state, has one of the lowest tax burdens in the OECD, and where unions have practically lost control over wage levels and structures? And why is it that Continental welfare states at similar levels of economic development, and with intermediate levels of tax burdens, should be doing so much less well?

The explanation is likely to be found in sectoral differences. Since the current debate focuses on international competitiveness, one might expect that—when compared to the non-taxed, deregulated, and de-unionized US economy—employment in European welfare states should be generally weak in sectors that are exposed to international competition.[4] By implication, then, European countries with high levels of employment should have achieved their success in the sheltered sectors of the economy. Unfortunately, this theoretically interesting distinction is not directly represented in the employment data available in the OECD Labour Force Statistics. Also, the boundary is shifting as hitherto sheltered jobs—for instance in telecommunications, financial services, or the construction industry—are becoming exposed to foreign competition with the completion of the European internal market and under the new WTO rules. Opting for the most comprehensive definition, I have included employment in all ISIC major divisions whose products are, actually or potentially, exported or subject to import competition. This includes not only all agricultural and industrial

[4] It is perhaps worth pointing out that, as used here, the definition of 'exposed sectors' does not depend on the greater or lesser *degree* of 'openness' of economies (i.e. the share of exports plus imports in GDP). Since competition works at the margin, it tends to affect the whole sector, even if only a small part of its product is internationally traded.

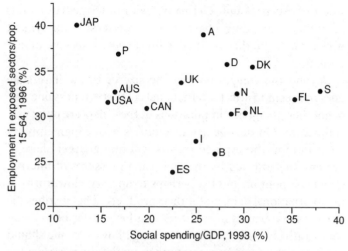

FIG. 4.2. Employment in the exposed sectors (ISIC 1–5, 7, 8)

employment, but also service employment in ISIC, divisions 7 ('Transport, Storage, and Communication') and 8 ('Financing, Insurance, Real Estate, and Business Services').

Taking these branches together, and focusing now more narrowly on the United States and the countries of the European Union, the pattern again seems to disappoint conventional expectations (Fig. 4.2). The overall statistical effect of the size of the welfare state on employment in the exposed sectors (1996 data) is extremely weak (and in fact slightly positive). Even more remarkable, the United States is not doing very well here, with an employment ratio of about 30 per cent—at the same level as France, and not much better than Ireland, the Netherlands, and Italy. By contrast, the Scandinavian countries with very large welfare states achieve higher employment ratios than the United States,

[129]

whereas Austria and Germany, with intermediate levels of welfare spending, have nearly the best employment performance in the internationally exposed sectors of the economy.[5]

Beyond the conclusion that the size of the welfare state does not seem to affect international competitiveness one way or another, the policy implications of these data are obviously ambivalent. On the one hand, countries with a high employment ratio in the exposed sectors will find a larger share of present jobs affected by the increasing pressures of international competition and by, perhaps temporary, downturns in the international demand for their products. That justifies the present nervousness in countries that have so far been doing comparatively well. On the other hand, however, one should not forget the more important other part of the message: the countries with the highest levels of employment in the internationally exposed sectors of the economy are characterized by stakeholder-oriented forms of corporate governance and by cooperative industrial relations that differ significantly from American (and British) forms of shareholder-oriented corporate governance and deregulated labour markets (Streeck 1992; Berger and Dore 1996; Crouch and Streeck 1997).

That does not mean that there is no need for reforms in countries with high employment ratios—as the intensity of international competition increases, employment in the exposed sectors can only be maintained if the speed of adjustment and innovation, and hence the flexibility of corporate and industrial governance, increases as well. However, in view of the superior competitiveness of the 'Rhine model'

---

[5] The employment ratios of Greece, Ireland, Spain, and Portugal include relatively more agricultural jobs than is true of the other countries.

(Albert 1993) in the international markets, it is hard to see what could be gained by throwing it out (even if that were politically feasible) in favour of Anglo-American models of market-driven corporate controls and industrial relations.

In any case, however, the data demonstrate that poor employment performance over the last decade cannot generally be ascribed to a loss of international competitiveness. It must also find its explanation in the sheltered sectors of the economy. Within the definition used here, these comprise the service branches in ISIC 6 ('Wholesale and Retail Trade, Restaurants and Hotels') and in ISIC 9 ('Community, Social, and Personal Services')—a heterogeneous collection which, however, shares the characteristic that local demand is being served by locally supplied services, and that foreign competition plays practically no role (Fig. 4.3).[6]

It is worthwhile therefore to explore further the factors underlying the association between local service employment and welfare spending. Since many of these services are in fact financed from either public or private sources, and may be provided either by public agencies or by non-profit organizations, by private professionals or by commercial firms, a further disaggregation along these lines may finally provide the explanation of different employment performances.

---

[6] That classification is questionable for employment in hotels and restaurants catering to tourists. While services are locally supplied, their consumers could opt for other locations. But tourism is not a separate category in OECD employment statistics, and the quantitative impact of the distortion seems to be limited. Countries that are strong in tourism do not seem to have exceptionally high employment ratios in local services.

[131]

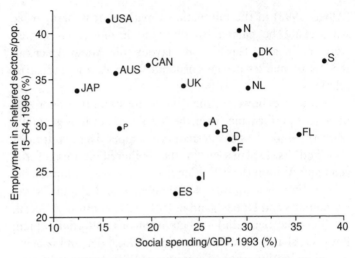

FIG. 4.3. Employment in sheltered sectors (ISIC 6 and 9)

4.1.3 Public and Private Services

Again, however, internationally comparable OECD data do not reflect all theoretically interesting dimensions. In particular, they do not distinguish between publicly or *privately financed* local services (which would directly correspond to welfare spending). The distinction that is possible is between employment in services *provided* by government agencies and services provided in the private sector.

As it turns out, this distinction does point to an explanation.[7] There is a strong negative ($r^2 = 0.46$) linear association

---

[7] Again, these data are not directly available, but they can be obtained by deducing OECD data on 'producers of government services' from data on total employment in divisions ISIC 6 plus ISIC 9. 'Employment in the private sector', as defined here, would thus include services performed by private physicians or by charities even if they are financed by the state or by social insurance funds.

[132]

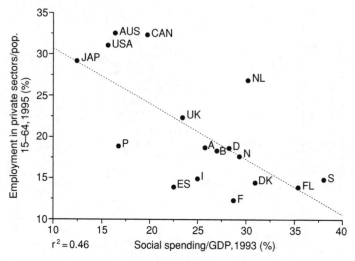

Fig. 4.4. Sheltered employment in the private sector

between welfare spending and local services provided in the private sector (Fig. 4.4). That it is not even stronger seems to be a consequence of the large part played by publicly financed (or at least publicly subsidized) but formally non-public charities in the provision of education, health care, and social services in some, but not all, countries included here. This probably explains the Dutch position far above, and the French location below, the regression line.

Employment in public services, by contrast, is positively and strongly ($r^2 = 0.52$) associated with welfare spending (Fig. 4.5). Employment ratios are by far the highest in Sweden and Denmark, and they are expectedly low in the United States. Public-sector employment is even lower in the Netherlands—where (publicly subsidized) charities play a large role not only in the social services but also in health care. In France, by contrast, public-sector services are stronger,

[133]

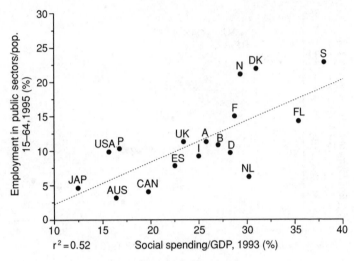

FIG. 4.5. Employment in the public sector

and private-sector services weaker, than expected. Belgium and Spain have low levels of employment in both sectors. Germany, finally, manages to have almost as little employment in private sector services as is true in Sweden, and to have a public sector that is exactly as 'lean' as is true in the United States.

The ambiguous pattern of employment in the sheltered sector as a whole is thus a composite result of two separate linear effects. In the United States and other countries with a small welfare state, local service jobs are created in the private sector of the economy, whereas in Denmark and Sweden with large welfare states, the public sector is able to provide high levels of local service employment. But why should the Continental welfare states with intermediate-size social expenditures have the worst of both worlds, instead of combining intermediate levels of employment, in the public and in the private sector, to achieve equally high overall levels of service employment?

4.2 SERVICE EMPLOYMENT AND THE WELFARE STATE

The explanation, I suggest, lies in differences in the structures of national welfare state and industrial relations systems. In order to simplify the argument, I will now concentrate on three models only, the American, the Scandinavian (represented by Sweden) and the Continental (represented by Germany), even though I know that there are significant differences among the Scandinavian welfare states, and even greater ones among the Continental systems, which need to be brought out by much more careful analyses than I could present here. In the American and Swedish cases, however, the explanations for their exceptionally high levels of employment in the sheltered service sectors are fairly straightforward.

4.2.1 The American Model

In the United States, generally low levels of taxation and the additional tax cuts of the 1980s have contributed to a highly unequal distribution of incomes (OECD 1995) which facilitated the simultaneous expansion of private service employment at the upper and at the lower end of the skill scale. Since education and health care are to a larger extent than elsewhere privately financed, the growing demand of affluent consumers for high-quality educational and medical services increases the number of well-paid jobs at the professional level. At the same time, the failure of Congress to raise the statutory

minimum wage, weak or non-existent unions, the short dura-
tion of unemployment benefits, and the virtual absence of
social assistance for the long-term unemployed have favoured
the emergence of a large low-wage labour market. This, in
turn, has facilitated the creation, or maintenance, of service
jobs in hotels, retail trade, restaurants, and a great variety of
other household and personal services. In these jobs, labour
productivity tends to be low. But since wages and taxes are
also very low, the American model allows large numbers of
low-skilled workers to find employment in the private sector.
As a matter of fact, in 1993–5, the share of low-wage employment was 25 per cent in the United States, as compared to
only 5.2 per cent in Sweden, 7.2 per cent in Belgium, and
between 12 and 13 per cent in most other Continental countries (OECD 1996a: table 3.2).[8] Thus, the upside of the
American model is the dynamic expansion of service employment at all qualification levels. Its downside is the plight of
the 'working poor' receiving incomes below the subsistence
level even when employed full time (Freeman 1995a; Weir
1995).[9]

4.2.2 The Scandinavian Model

In Sweden and Denmark, by contrast, very high taxes, strong
unions, and generous rates of income replacement in case of

---

[8] In the OECD study, low-paid workers are defined as full-time workers
who earn less than two-thirds of median earnings for all full-time workers
(OECD 1995: 69).

[9] It should be emphasized, however, that the United States already has
a federal programme, the 'Earned Income Tax Credit' which, if adequately
funded, would be well suited to deal with the inadequate incomes of the
'working poor' (Haveman 1997).

unemployment have reduced income inequality and wage differentials to the lowest level among OECD countries. At the same time, education and health care are publicly financed and publicly provided. As a consequence, there is neither a low-wage labour market nor much room for private services at the professional level. Instead, high levels of tax revenue are used to finance universal health services and education as well as a wide range of free social services for families with young children, for the elderly, the handicapped, and the sick, for drug addicts and immigrants.[10] These services not only involve work for highly trained professionals but also provide a large number of decently paid jobs for persons with relatively low levels of formal training.

The obvious downside of the Swedish model is its dependence on very high levels of taxation which have become vulnerable to increasing international tax competition for mobile capital, and to the growing tax resistance of mobile professionals (Freeman 1995*b*). Thus the need for fiscal retrenchment in the 1990s forced governments to reduce not only the generosity of welfare payments, but also the level of public-sector employment—with the consequence that unemployment has risen to normal European levels, even though the level of employment continues to be very high by international standards. In Denmark, however, employment has held up remarkably well even in the 1990s.

---

[10] In 1993, Sweden spent 6.39% of GDP on services for elderly and disabled people and on family services. In Denmark, the percentage was 4.36, and in Finland 3.01. The level is much lower in the Netherlands (1.16%), in France (1.11%), and in the UK (1.05%), and lower still in West Germany (0.74%) and Ireland (0.53%). Expenditure on these services is minimal in Belgium (0.36%), Italy (0.30%), Spain (0.20%), and Portugal (0.13%), and practically non-existent in Greece (OECD 1996*b*).

4.2.3 The Continental Unemployment Trap

The more highly developed Continental welfare states, with the notable exception of the Netherlands, have not been able to achieve high levels of local services in either the public or the private sector. In contrast to the United States, however, their levels of employment in the public sector cannot simply be explained by the smaller size of the welfare state. While it is true that total social spending amounts to more than 37 per cent in Sweden, whereas Continental welfare states tend to absorb only between 25 and 30 per cent of GDP, that is still much more than the 15 per cent share of social spending in the United States (OECD 1996*b*). If nevertheless public-sector employment in Germany is exactly as low as it is in the United States, that appears as a path-dependent consequence of the Bismarckian model of the welfare state, which was originally meant to deal only with the social risks arising if the single (male) breadwinner was unable to support his family through full-time work (Esping-Andersen 1990). Hence, Continental welfare states provide quite generous transfer payments in cases of disability, retirement, and unemployment—but they never developed a Scandinavian commitment to social services that would complement or compete with the functions performed in the family by mothers, wives, and daughters (see n. 10, above). As a consequence, the Continental welfare state does not create much employment in publicly financed social services.

There are of course well-paid professional jobs in public education and in publicly financed health care provided in public hospitals or in private practice. But the fact that these services are publicly financed, from tax revenues or from social insurance funds, implies that employment growth is held back or even reversed by efforts to reduce tax burdens and public-sector budget deficits, whereas employment in the

United States will dynamically expand as affluent consumers are increasing their demand for high-quality services in education and health care in the private sector.[11]

In the private sector, service employment at the upper end of the labour market is held back in Continental welfare states since education and health care are largely provided free of charge. Even when the quality and quantity of publicly financed services are unsatisfactory, consumers will hesitate to switch to privately supplied services for which—in addition to their tax bill—they would have to pay prices covering the full cost of production. Hence high-quality private services are more or less confined to the niches of luxury markets.

At the lower end of the labour market, however, the Continental welfare state is as effective as its Scandinavian counterpart in destroying the viability of low-wage service jobs in the private sector. Compared to the United States, at any rate, levels of taxation are high, unions are strong, income inequality and wage differentials are low,[12] and reservation wages are defined by relatively generous wage replacement in case of unemployment and indefinitely available social assistance payments. Hence the American problem of the 'working poor' with full-time jobs at wages below the subsistence level could not arise in either the Scandinavian or the Continental welfare states. But in avoiding that problem, the Continental

[11] Moreover, since American state universities are also charging high tuition fees, even public-sector employment is able to expand as a consequence of rising private demand.

[12] In 1993, the ratio of median wages (for men and women) to wages in the lowest decile (D5/D1) was 2.05 in the USA, 1.79 in the UK, 1.75 in Italy, 1.65 in Japan, 1.64 in France, 1.54 in the Netherlands, 1.44 in Germany, 1.43 in Belgium, and 1.34 in Sweden. Germany, incidentally, is practically the only OECD country where wage differentials have continuously *fallen* between 1983 and 1993 (OECD 1995: table 3.1).

model is actually destroying more employment opportunities in the private sector than is even true in Scandinavian welfare states.

The reason is that Continental welfare states are primarily financed through payroll taxes. In Germany, for instance, 74 per cent of total expenditures was financed through workers' and employers' contributions to social insurance systems in 1991, and in France that was true of 82 per cent. In Germany, these contributions at present amount to more than 42 per cent of the total wage paid by the employer. By contrast, Scandinavian welfare states are to a larger extent financed from general tax revenues which, in 1991, amounted to 83 per cent of total social spending in Denmark, leaving only 17 per cent to be paid as surcharge on wages (BMA 1995).

The dependence on payroll taxes makes Continental welfare states particularly vulnerable to any increase in unemployment which increases expenditures and reduces revenues at the same time. As a consequence, it then becomes necessary either to reduce benefits at a time when more persons become dependent upon them, or to raise payroll taxes at a time when firms are particularly sensitive to any increase in labour costs. Neither of these options is politically easy to implement. Moreover, there is now a widespread belief that social insurance contributions, collected in the form of payroll taxes, are themselves a major cause of high levels of unemployment. By raising the price of labour, so it is argued, they reduce international competitiveness and contribute to the replacement of labour by capital.

From an economic point of view, however, not all of these arguments are well founded. If the price of labour were generally raised by social insurance contributions, the effect on international competitiveness would be neutralized by a fall in the exchange rate—and if devaluation were prevented by monetary policy, the lack of competitiveness would have to show in the form of a persistent trade deficit. Since neither of these effects seems to have been generally true for Continental welfare states over the last decade (OECD 1997a), it is reasonable to think that the impact of social insurance contributions on the cost of labour has been internalized, together with all other factors affecting the cost of production, in the normal processes of wage-setting (Härtel 1997).[13] As a consequence, the take-home pay of workers in countries that rely largely on payroll taxes will be lower than it would otherwise have been.

All that, however, is true only at the middle and upper ranges of the labour market, whereas things are very different at the lower end of the pay scale. Here, the availability of social assistance defines a lower threshold below which net wages cannot be reduced. Thus, certain types of 'bad jobs', which are economically viable in the United States, simply could not exist in Europe—which is, of course, a fully intended effect of European welfare states. But what is probably not intended is the impact of payroll taxes on jobs well above the subsistence level.

If the net wage of the worker cannot fall below a guaranteed minimum, the consequence is that any social insurance contributions, payroll taxes, and wage taxes that are levied on jobs at the lower end of the pay scale will not be absorbed by the employee but must be added to the total labour cost borne by the employer. In Germany, that would amount to a surcharge (social insurance contributions plus wage tax) of at

---

[13] This is not meant to deny that *increases* in the rate of social insurance contributions will have negative effects on employment, since the downward adjustment of wages will take time, especially if the rate of inflation is very low.

least 50 per cent. Assuming that additional overhead costs will be proportional to total labour cost, the implication is that the minimum productivity that a job must reach in order to be viable in the market is raised by more than 50 per cent above the level that would be required if labour costs were equal to the net reservation wage of the worker. As a consequence, a considerable range of perfectly decent jobs which, in the absence of payroll taxes, would be commercially viable are eliminated from the private labour market of Continental welfare states. In this sense, therefore, it is indeed fair to say that Continental welfare states are causing high levels of long-term unemployment for persons with low levels of marketable skills.

4.2.4 Continental Options

If the downside of the American model is the plight of the working poor, and if the Scandinavian model has become highly vulnerable to the erosion of its tax base, Continental welfare states suffer from their inability to expand domestic-service employment either in the public or in the private sector. In the abstract, one might think that the Continental employment gap might be closed by moving either in the American or in the Scandinavian direction. If both options were equally feasible, political preferences would diverge widely. Practically speaking, however, the Scandinavian option appears to be out of the question. The reasons are financial and political. Continental welfare states, even though less expensive than their Scandinavian counterparts, are already hard-pressed financially. Thus, a Scandinavian-type service expansion would either require substantial tax increases or further reductions of welfare transfers; at the same time, there is no large and well-organized political demand for additional public services, whereas the political opposition to either tax increases or further cutbacks in social transfers is already highly mobilized. In fact, a Scandinavian solution is not even discussed on the left, whereas the 'American way' is strongly advocated by business associations and neoliberal parties demanding to cut social assistance to the bone. In most Continental states, however, unions and political parties committed to the 'Rhine model' are able and willing to block the radical dismantling of the welfare state as well.

Nevertheless, it is possible to specify, at least in the abstract, strategies through which Continental welfare states could help to create, rather than to destroy, private employment in local services. To be effective, such strategies must address the specific problems of low-skill groups—and if the solution is to be found in the private sector, that implies that European countries must actively promote the creation of a low-wage labour market, which does not exist at present. In order to be normatively acceptable and politically feasible, however, European solutions cannot allow the emergence of a large underclass of the 'working poor'. Hence low-wage jobs, European style, would still need to provide net incomes well above the subsistence level defined by social-assistance rules.

If the problem is defined in this fashion, the solution seems to require a reorientation of the welfare state from providing full income support for persons who are full-time unemployed to providing partial income support for persons working at wages below the present minimum level. The most comprehensive solution could be achieved by a fundamental reorganization of the welfare state along the lines of a negative income tax—which is presently discussed in Germany under the name of 'Bürgergeld' (Mitschke 1985; 1995). It would replace all present forms of means-tested social transfer payments by a single payment that decreases at a rate of, say, 50 per cent as income from work (or other sources) increases.[14] As a consequence, part-time or low-wage employment would become economically attractive for present welfare recipients, and employers would have incentives to create a wide range of economically viable employment opportunities at the lower end of the labour market.

By its own logic, however, the negative income tax would require a far-reaching restructuring of the present systems of taxation, social assistance, social insurance, pensions, and wage-setting. Moreover, the available estimates of its overall financial consequences are still enormously divergent.[15] Thus, chances are slim that Continental welfare states could soon be reorganized in this fundamental fashion. Many of these difficulties could be avoided, however, by more modest, less costly, and simpler proposals that would focus exclusively on job creation, rather than attempting a fundamental reorganization of the welfare state. Such solutions would simply provide income subsidies to workers in low-wage jobs below the present effective minimum, and leave all other present rules as they are (Scharpf 1993). In both versions, however, the employment effect of income subsidies would depend on the cooperation of unions that would have to agree

[14] The negative income tax, like the Earned Income Tax Credit in the United States and similar schemes in the UK and in Ireland, would be oriented toward family or household incomes—which is not the optimal criterion from a purely employment-oriented perspective.

[15] A major cost factor results from the fact that the lower threshold of income taxation will shift from the present subsistence level to twice that amount. Beyond that, the estimates are highly sensitive to assumptions about how the higher threshold should be treated throughout the tax scale, and about which present transfers are to be replaced by the negative income tax. As a consequence, estimates of net costs (in the absence of any employment effects) vary between zero and close to DM 200 billion (Hüther 1990; DIW 1996).

to the creation of new wage scales below the present minimum level. That is not an attractive function for unions that see their mission in raising, rather than lowering, minimum wages. Moreover, unions fear that wage reductions at the lower end could induce a general erosion of the present wage structure (Hanesch 1995). Even though that objection may not be plausible in economic theory, it has so far prevented political parties in Germany from adopting proposals of this nature.

In the light of these difficulties, a functionally equivalent solution, which would not depend on the active cooperation of the unions, might appear more promising. Its feasibility rests on precisely those features of the Continental welfare states that are so damaging to service employment, i.e. their dependence on social insurance contributions from employers and workers as a major source of welfare finance. In Germany, for example, they amount at present to more than 42 per cent of the employer's wage bill, and they are shared equally between employers' and workers' contributions. Hence, if these contributions were (almost) completely waived at and below the present minimum wage of about DM 10 per hour, the wage bill of the employer would be reduced by 22 per cent—which would increase the profitability of service employment by the same percentage.[16] At the same time, the take-home pay of the worker would also increase by the same percentage—which would increase the attractiveness of low-end jobs and, perhaps, would also make jobs below the present minimum wage more attractive.

---

[16] A more far-reaching proposal following the same logic has been presented by Jean-Paul Fitoussi (1994): it would relieve employers of the social insurance contributions required at the level of the minimum wage, for *all* *workers* at present employed.

[145]

Of course, these jobs would still need to be fully covered by the social insurance system. Hence, the contributions waived would have to be made up by payments financed from general tax revenues. Like the negative income tax, the size of the subsidy would have to decrease at higher wage levels. Thus, one might eliminate contributions almost totally at and below the level of the present minimum wage, and the subsidy could again be reduced to zero at twice that level. But these are matters for political judgement and compromise, which would have to vary from one country to another. In principle, however, this solution should be open to all countries that are financing very large shares of their social expenditure through non-wage labour costs.

In conclusion, I suggest, the Continental employment gap does not primarily result from a loss of international competitiveness. It primarily affects the sheltered sector; it is caused not by the size of the welfare state, but by its characteristic structure and mode of financing; and these causes could be remedied by institutional reforms that would increase, rather than destroy, the level of social-policy support for disadvantaged groups in Continental societies. Moreover, to the extent that unemployment could be transformed into subsidized employment in the private sector, the fiscal pressures on the welfare state would also be reduced.[17]

---

[17] Quantitative estimates of the employment effect of the negative income tax and similar schemes are not available, and for good reasons: in order to be effective, these programmes must change the present structures of labour markets—hence simulation models validated by time series data reflecting past and existing structures cannot be used to predict their effects. At the most, it might be possible to estimate how many, and which, currently existing jobs would be lost in the United States if the US labour market were truncated at the *de facto* minimum wage that is at present effective in Germany.

4.3 RESISTING THE EROSION OF THE TAX BASE

However, even if the size of the welfare state does not impair the international competitiveness of national producers, international competition among regulatory systems does challenge the viability of advanced welfare states because it also undermines the national capacity to collect revenue from mobile tax bases. There is a premium, therefore, on revenue systems that are less vulnerable to international mobility.

Seen purely from the perspective of tax competition, Continental systems financed largely from payroll taxes appear in fact quite robust.[18] Because of their perceived insurance character, social-security contributions may also be less likely to provoke tax resistance than, say, income taxes. Moreover, since the ultimate incidence even of employers' contributions is likely to be on the take-home pay of the worker, they should also be less vulnerable to the pressures of tax competition for mobile factors of production.[19] Thus, if reforms of welfare finance are considered at all, they might emphasize the insurance character even more by eliminating employers'

---

[18] That does not invalidate the conclusion that, *from the perspective of international competition in product markets*, welfare states that depend primarily on non-wage labour costs are at a comparative disadvantage (Scharpf 1997*b*: 31). The implication is that economic integration creates different types of regulatory competition (regarding product markets, investment markets, and tax revenues) among nation states that may lead to contradictory conclusions with regard to the relative robustness of specific policy instruments.

[19] That conclusion may seem overly optimistic in light of the persistent political campaign of employers and business associations against the high level of non-wage labour costs in Germany and other Continental countries. Conceivably, business decisions may be as much affected by a 'tax illusion' as Keynes thought that wage-setting was affected by a 'money illusion'.

contributions altogether, and by moving from systems that insure only workers toward the Swiss model of universal and compulsory individual insurance—which would also have the effect of reducing the contributions paid by individual workers, who are at present required to pay for the insurance of the non-working population as well.[20] Changes in that direction would in effect immunize those parts of the welfare state that assure income support in cases of sickness, disability, and old age against the competitive pressures of an internationalized economy. Insurance contributions, even if required by law, would assume the character of private investment or consumption expenditures, rather than of public burdens on the economy.

However, if the insurance elements of social security are emphasized more, that would leave a larger part of redistributive transfers to be financed from general tax revenues. As discussed before, the vulnerability to international competition is greatest for taxes on capital incomes, business taxes, and taxes on the personal incomes of internationally mobile professionals. Many countries are responding to these pressures by reducing nominal rates of personal and corporate income taxes. Yet even if revenue losses may be partly compensated if tax exemptions are eliminated at the same time, the steering effect of the tax system and its perceived distributive justice will suffer. Beyond that, the main choice for European welfare states seems to be between either reducing benefits and services or shifting the financial burden from taxes on profits and capital incomes to less mobile tax bases.

---

[20] As is true for health insurance in Switzerland, contributions from persons with low incomes could then be subsidized from general tax revenues (Alber and Bernardi-Schenkluhn 1991).

On average, the effective tax rates on the less mobile income from labour and on consumption expenditures have risen substantially since the early 1970s throughout the OECD (Garrett 1998),[21] and even now, consumption taxes—including taxes on energy input, on pollution, and other 'green' taxes—seem to represent the favourite solution for governments and political parties that are committed to defending the welfare state.[22] These taxes have the dual advantages of being difficult to avoid even for the owners of highly mobile assets and, if applied in the form of a value-added tax, of affecting imports as much as local production, and not burdening exports.[23] But consumption taxes are also associated with two disadvantages. First, at uniform rates their distributive impact tends to be regressive since poor people spend larger shares of their incomes than rich people. Hence countries that already depend heavily on consumption taxes tend to have split tax rates—high for 'luxury goods' and low for 'basic needs'.[24] Second, and more important in the present

[21] Geoffrey Garrett also reports a rise in the effective rates of capital taxation, from which he concludes that globalization and international mobility did not reduce the capacity of governments to tax capital incomes. To the extent that the effect is real, it may indeed be explained by the fact that those countries that have reduced marginal rates the most have also broadened their tax bases. But since Garrett's definition of capital taxes includes taxes on totally immobile real estate (and since the property tax plays a very large role in Anglo-American tax systems), the effect of increased international mobility cannot really be tested with Garrett's data.

[22] Given the large reliance of the United States, Britain, and other Anglo-Saxon countries on the property tax, and its virtual insignificance everywhere else, it seems remarkable that this non-mobile tax base has not yet found more political attention.

[23] Within the European Community, that is of course only true as long as the 'country-of-destination principle' is still in force.

[24] Discussion on the more radical option of replacing the progressive income tax by a progressive 'cash flow' tax on expenditures is not suffi-

context, high rates of value-added taxes will eliminate low-productive service employment just as effectively from the 'official' labour market as is true for high payroll taxes. Hence it would also be necessary to reduce or eliminate the value-added tax on services produced by low-wage labour. However, both of these forms of 'positive discrimination' are difficult to define and also difficult to implement efficiently.

The second option, which so far has not been actively explored in Europe, concerns the financing of infrastructure facilities and services that are at present provided free of charge, or with heavy subsidies, by the public sector.[25] Many of these—e.g. secondary and higher education or museums and opera houses—are predominantly used by medium- and higher-income groups whose income-tax burden is being reduced as a consequence of international tax competition and political tax resistance. At the same time, however, high-quality universities, cultural facilities, or medical services have become even more important for maintaining, or increasing, the economic attractiveness of regions exposed to international competition. Hence, cutting back on these services under the pressures of international competition, as is currently happening in European welfare states, is likely to be self-defeating in economic terms. The same is true of much of the public infrastructure, and of essential public services.

In some of these areas, like telecommunications, air transport, and perhaps super-highways, privatization may be the perfect answer; in others like waste removal and the construc-

ciently advanced in Europe to allow an estimate of its desirability and political feasibility.

[25] Perhaps the decision of the new Labour government in Britain to charge substantial student fees may initiate the search for such solutions in other service fields as well.

tion and maintenance of residential roads, cost-covering user charges have long been used and are considered unproblematic. Still other services, for instance public security and crime prevention, may have the character of 'club goods' at the level of local communities which, if financed transparently by local taxes, will encounter little taxpayer resistance. Others, like national defence, are in the nature of 'pure public goods' that must be financed from general tax revenues if they are to be provided at all.

But that still leaves a wide range of facilities and services providing 'private goods' that are of great value to those who use them, but which are also important to the social, cultural, and economic viability of advanced industrial societies (i.e. they have positive externalities). Nevertheless, they are not used by everybody, or not by everybody all the time, and they tend to be used more frequently and more intensively by high-income groups. At the same time, the full cost of their provision is so high that low-income groups would be unable to afford these services even if a negative income tax or similar redistributive schemes were in place. In European welfare states, the traditional response to this distributive constellation has been to provide high-quality services to everybody free of charge, or at heavily subsidized user charges, and to rely on progressive income taxes in order to make high-income groups pay a disproportionate share of their cost.

As this form of financing is eroding under the pressure of international tax competition, and is losing its normative plausibility as national tax systems are becoming more regressive, one of two scenarios seems possible. In the first, financial constraints will reduce the quantity and quality of public services. On the one hand, publicly financed or subsidized facilities may be closed down, and levels of service may be reduced to such an extent that the ideal of universal

[151]

access to quality libraries, museums, theatre, opera, and concert performances, swimming pools and sports facilities, or public transport is abandoned. What will take their place, then, are commercial facilities serving luxury markets or catering either to the highly concentrated demand in a few metropolitan centres (as is true on Broadway) or to the common tastes of mass audiences.[26] On the other hand, the quality of public services that are maintained may suffer to such an extent that they will become a 'poor man's' option while the rich will prefer to emigrate to expensive private schools, private universities, and private medical practice.

Much of this is happening already, and not all of it is unacceptable. But where it is considered unacceptable, a second scenario needs to be explored that aims at maintaining the ideal of universally available high-quality services by shifting a larger part of their financial support from general tax revenues to means-tested user charges. The logic is simple: if high-income groups are no longer willing to pay the high taxes that could support free services, they could at least be made to pay the full cost of those services that they are in fact using. Social justice could then be maintained by providing means-tested vouchers for low- and medium-income families that could not afford to pay full-cost user charges.[27] An attractive side effect of such voucher systems

---

[26] It is true that electronic media are now able to provide highly specialized information and entertainment services to dispersed audiences that could not previously have supported commercial programmes catering to their tastes or needs. But that covers only a relatively small range of the classical functions of public services and infrastructure facilities.

[27] If it is thought to be a problem that university students should be made dependent on their families, vouchers could be made available to all (qualified) students, but recipients might be required to pay a lifelong surcharge on their income tax which, on average, would correspond to the cost of the voucher.

would be the strong element of consumer power and quality competition that is introduced into the governance of education and other public service sectors if users are allowed to choose between public and private service providers (as is at present becoming true for public and private schools in Switzerland).

To summarize: there is reason to expect that increasing constraints on the national capacity to tax will affect the viability of European welfare states. Nevertheless, the values served by the welfare state may be defended by a shift from highly vulnerable sources of revenue to modes of finance that are more robust against the pressures of economic competition. Depending on the existing mix of transfers and services, and existing patterns of finance, optimal solutions would surely differ from one country to another. Nevertheless, it should be worthwhile in most countries to emphasize differentiated consumption taxes for the collection of general revenue, to emphasize individual insurance for the financing of income-maintaining transfers, and to emphasize means-tested user charges for the financing of public services. These suggestions are not meant as patent solutions, and they certainly would not be easy to adopt and implement, but they are meant to show that the democratic welfare state is not condemned to abdicate, or to organize its own dismantling, even if the hope for its reconstruction through positive integration at the European level should not be fulfilled.

In this chapter, I have discussed all of the problem areas identified at the end of the preceding chapter, except for industrial relations. One reason is that I am not sufficiently knowledgeable to dispute the deep pessimism of authors who have long studied and thought deeply about the changing conditions in this field (Visser and Ebbinghaus 1992; Streeck 1997b). What I could add is the observation, based on the employment data presented above, that apparently the most highly institutionalized ('corporatist') industrial relations systems have not been doing badly at all in terms of maintaining high levels of employment in the internationally exposed sectors of the economy (Rhodes 1996; Neubäumer 1997). If this were more generally realized, perhaps political campaigns against the institutional 'rigidities' of corporatist industrial relations would appear less justified by the pressures of international economic competition.

That is not meant to suggest that the corporatist model of highly institutionalized 'cooperative' industrial relations should be generally superior, under present conditions, to the Anglo-American model of deregulated labour markets, shareholder-oriented corporate governance, and highly decentralized wage negotiations (Streeck 1995a; 1997b; Crouch and Streeck 1997). It seems more likely that both of these models are able to succeed reasonably well in a highly competitive international environment (OECD 1997d). But what of countries in which industrial-relations institutions have not been weakened to the extent that is true in the United States and in Britain, but are also not 'cooperative' to the extent that is possible in Sweden, Denmark, Austria, Germany, or the Netherlands? For them, one might expect serious difficulties—especially if they should become members of the European Monetary Union. Given a uniform rate of inflation throughout the EMU, countries where the rise of unit labour costs exceeds the current rate of inflation are bound to suffer competitive disadvantages that will increase unemployment in the exposed sectors. Countries with corporatist institutions are, in principle, capable of influencing wage-setting to avoid such consequences (Scharpf 1991; Rhodes 1996; Garrett 1998); and presumably purely market-driven systems can do so as well. The critical question for other countries then seems to be whether they will be able to change their existing industrial-relations institutions in one or the other of these directions. But these questions cannot be pursued further here.

CHAPTER 5

The European Contribution

In the last chapter, I have tried to show that national governments are not helpless in those crucial policy areas where existing solutions are constrained by the legal prohibitions of negative integration, or by the economic pressures of regulatory and tax competition in the integrated market. It remains true, however, that the more robust national solutions that were discussed would require far-reaching and deep-cutting institutional reforms on a scale that can only be compared to the radical changes that were brought about by the Conservative government in Britain. But eighteen years of single-party rule are hard to imagine in other European countries—in many of which, moreover, multi-party government coalitions, federalism, corporatism, judicial review, and central-bank independence create many more 'veto points' in the political process than is true in Britain (Tsebelis 1995). Hence even if national solutions were available in principle, it is unlikely that they could be speedily adopted and implemented everywhere.

In any case, high and rising levels of mass unemployment, tightening fiscal constraints, and the growing pressure of political dissatisfaction and, in some countries, political radicalization are not generally conducive to the longer-term perspective required by institutional reforms of a fundamental nature. Moreover, even if national policy makers were not incapacitated by internal conflicts and the myopia of crisis politics, they would still be struggling, as it were, with one arm tied behind their backs, by the legal constraints of

European competition policy and by the regulatory competition against other member states—both of which tend to create comparative advantages, in domestic politics, to political parties and interests favouring the dismantling, rather than the reconstruction, of welfare state institutions. Thus, policy analyses guided by an interest in defending the social achievements of the post-war decades even under the conditions of globalized markets and European economic integration must still explore the possibilities of European contributions to more effective problem-solving.

However, as was to be expected on the basis of analyses in Chapter 2 above, the Treaty of Amsterdam has done little to increase the institutional capacity for 'positive integration' and effective European problem-solving in the face of unresolved conflicts of interest or of ideology among member governments. The President of the Commission, it is true, will be strengthened by having a voice in the appointment of commissioners, and the European Parliament is strengthened by a considerable expansion of the items on which it has an effective veto under the co-decision procedure. But no agreement has been achieved with regard to voting rules in the Council of Ministers—instead, even countries like Germany and France, which in the past have promoted majoritarian decision rules, now seem to have become more concerned about the risk of being outvoted in an enlarged Community.

Nevertheless, in view of the problems discussed in this book, the Amsterdam Summit produced some compromises that represent moves in the right direction—forward on employment policy and backward (or more cautiously forward) on negative integration. After considering the possible implications of these agreements, I will then turn to European options not discussed, or not accepted, at Amsterdam— which, however, are of a kind that should be sufficiently

[157]

compatible with the interests of national governments to make further consideration worthwhile.

5.1 COORDINATED NATIONAL ACTION ON EMPLOYMENT?

The Amsterdam agreements on employment have generally been criticized as compromises on the level of the lowest common denominator, or as exercises in symbolic politics (Wolter and Hasse 1997). They have certainly disappointed those among their promoters who had hoped for a commitment to Keynesian full-employment policies, pursued through Community programmes initiating large-scale infrastructure investments. But what was agreed upon may in fact have more positive implications than a return to the deficit-spending philosophy of the 1970s could have had.

A 'New Title on Employment' will now be included in the Treaty of the European Communities. Its Art. 125 commits the member states to 'work towards developing a coordinated strategy for employment'; Art. 126 defines 'promoting employment as a matter of common concern', and Art. 128 requires each member state to provide the Council and the Commission with an 'annual report on the principal measures taken to implement its employment policy'—on the basis of which the Council may 'make recommendations to Member States'. Moreover, the Council will establish an 'Employment Committee' that is to 'monitor the employment situation and employment policies' in the member states and to formulate opinions in preparation of Council proceedings. Taken together, these provisions hold three important promises.

First, by declaring national employment policies a matter of common concern of all member states, and by creating the organizational and procedural conditions for monitoring and evaluation, the Amsterdam Treaty may, for the first time, provide some safeguards against the temptation of all countries to protect domestic jobs through 'beggar-my-neighbour' policies, competitive deregulation, and tax cuts. In the past, certainly, European governments have observed and responded to each others' moves: if Britain deregulated labour markets, the Netherlands extended the limits on temporary employment, and Germany eliminated employment security in firms with ten or fewer employees. Similarly, when France chose to reduce employers' contributions to social insurance, Germany and Sweden cut sick pay, and Germany is now lowering pension levels and requiring patients to bear part of their health care expenses in order to reduce non-wage labour costs. If others then respond again, all players in the European competitiveness game may find themselves at lower levels of social protection without having improved their relative position. While I am not suggesting that all of these competitive stratagems should have been prevented, it nevertheless could have been very useful to have them examined internationally.

Second, the commitment to compare and evaluate national policies with a view to sharing information about 'best practices', and to promoting 'innovative approaches' (Art. 129), creates conditions that are conducive to the joint discussion of structures and causes of employment problems, and to the joint exploration of employment policy options at the national level. Since these discussions in the reconstituted 'Employment Committee' of the Council will be more detached from immediate political pressures and acute crises than is true of national politics, there is a hope that innovative solutions to common problems could be worked out that would not have been found in the rough-and-tumble of competitive party politics dominating national policy processes. Given an active role of the Commission, and opportunities for 'deliberative'

interactions in a permanent committee of senior civil servants, there is at least a chance that an understanding of the
causes of the 'European employment gap', and of potentially
effective employment strategies, could emerge that goes beyond the ubiquitous recipes of the OECD *Jobs Study* (1994),
for labour market deregulation, public-sector retrenchment,
and the reduction of social benefits.

Last, but by no means least, the explicit postulation of an
employment goal, coequal with the fundamental commitment
to the four freedoms of the internal market, may have beneficial effects against the dominance of neoliberal interpretations
of what European integration is about in the practice of the
Commission and in the decisions of the European Court of
Justice. At any rate, it will now be harder to argue that, as
a matter of positive law, the Community should be strictly
limited to achieving, and protecting, the 'four freedoms' and
undistorted market competition (Mestmäcker 1987; 1994). In
this regard, it may also help that the Treaty now refers to the
full set of fundamental rights guaranteed by the 1950 European Convention for the Protection of Human Rights and
Fundamental Freedoms and it now includes a more explicit
commitment to 'a high level of protection and improvement
of the quality of the environment'. What is to be hoped for, in
other words, is a reconsideration of the legal scope of negative
integration in the light of social and political goals other than
the maximization of market competition.

5.2 LIMITS ON NEGATIVE INTEGRATION

As a matter of fact, Amsterdam has taken some explicit steps
in that direction, and there have also been Council directives
and decisions of the European Court of Justice which have
had the effect of limiting the reach of negative integration in

order to protect national solutions that could otherwise be challenged as violating the prohibition of non-tariff barriers to trade, as interfering with the free movement of services, or as competition-distorting state aids or regulations.

Amsterdam Agreements

At the Amsterdam Summit itself, some sort of agreement was reached on three of the issues arising from the extension of European competition law into service areas 'affected with a public interest' that I discussed in Chapter 2, above. The first, and potentially most far-reaching, will insert a new Art. 16 in the Treaty whose delicately diplomatic formulations are worth being quoted in full:

Without prejudice to Articles 73, 86 and 87, and given the place occupied by services of general economic interest in the shared values of the Union as well as their role in promoting social and territorial cohesion, the Community and the Member States, each within their respective powers and within the scope of application of this Treaty, shall take care that such services operate on the basis of principles and conditions which enable them to fulfil their missions.

Variants of this clause had long been promoted by public-service associations (Villeneuve 1997) and the French government. On the face of it, it seems to lack any operative content—which may be due to political disagreement among member governments over the legitimate scope of a *service public* exemption from European competition law. But even if the European Council had been of one mind, it would have been difficult to constrain the scope of negative integration in a general way. Since the Commission and the Court had extended that scope in a case-by-case process of individual decisions, each of which was accepted and implemented as the law of the land by the governments immediately affected,

[161]

the Council could neither enact a wholesale reversal of past decisions nor could it formulate a clear-cut rule that would satisfy, for an unknown variety of future cases, the equally legitimate interests in reducing economic protectionism and in protecting the substantive 'missions' of various *service public* institutions. Since the relative importance of these potentially conflicting concerns must be determined with a view to the specific circumstances of concrete cases, the Council could only signal to the Commission, the Court,[1] and the legal profession that—in light of the 'shared values of the Union'—more weight ought to be given to the purposes served by public-service missions. Whether that signal will be respected or ignored is largely beyond the Council's control.[2]

The Amsterdam Summit sent a similar signal by its 'Protocol to the TEC' regarding public-service broadcasting which, rather than amending the text of the Treaty, reminds Commission and Court that 'the system of public broadcasting in the Member States is directly related to the democratic, social and cultural needs of each society', and then goes on to formulate 'interpretative provisions' according to which the Treaty does not rule out the funding of public-service broad-

---

[1] That the message is indeed intended for the Court is also made clear by a 'Declaration to the Final Act' which stipulates that 'The provisions of Article 16 on public services shall be implemented with full respect for the jurisprudence of the Court of Justice, inter alia as regards the principles of *equality of treatment, quality and continuity of such services*'—principles, that is, which the Court itself had on occasion accepted as justification for *limiting* the reach of European competition law.

[2] There is, of course, the possibility that national governments might influence the Commission by twisting the arms of 'their' commissioners and the members of their cabinets (S. Schmidt 1997). But that option was always considered highly inappropriate (Ross 1995), and it will become less effective, now that the President of the Commission must agree to the appointment (and reappointment!) of individual commissioners.

casting. Again, however, the assertion is qualified by the proviso 'that such funding does not affect trading conditions and competition in the Community to an extent which would be contrary to the common interest'.

The same is true in the third instance of a 'Declaration to the Final Act' in which the Intergovernmental Conference notes that 'the Community's existing competition rules' are not violated by the existence of, and the facilities granted to, public credit institutions in Germany—an assertion which once more is followed by the qualification that such 'facilities may not adversely affect the conditions of competition to an extent beyond that required' by the infrastructure functions of these institutions. In other words, the Commission and the Court will retain their role in balancing competing principles in specific cases, but they have now been alerted to the importance of some of the countervailing values to be considered. That effect should not be underestimated—but it is far removed from a reassertion of direct 'intergovernmental' control over the functions delegated to the Commission and the Court of Justice. In the field of negative integration, these 'agents' will continue to play their 'supranational' roles (Garrett 1995*b*; Mattli and Slaughter 1995), but they do so in the context of a political discourse with governments and the Council over the proper performance of that role.

Council Directives

In areas where hard and fast rules can be defined, it is of course possible to limit the impact of negative integration more directly through the adoption of Council directives—provided that the Commission is willing to take the initiative, and that the directive is not blocked through conflicts of interest among member governments within the Council itself. An example is the 'posted workers directive' (96/71/EC) adopted after many years of negotiations in December 1996. It deals with a paradoxical problem of labour mobility that could only arise after the Single Market programme had also effectuated the guarantees of free movement for services. Whereas the free movement of workers had previously given rise to numerous directives and court decisions entitling foreign workers to wages and social rights equal to those of national workers *at the place of work* (Ireland 1995; Tsoukalis 1997: ch. 6), the new freedom of cross-border service provision was now to be realized under the ground rules of 'mutual recognition'—meaning that service firms could operate anywhere in the Community under the regulations *of their home country*. The logical implication was that firms (and even individual workers operating as independent contractors) could provide services abroad while applying the wage rates and social insurance rules of their country of origin—conditions that were particularly attractive to firms located in Portugal, Britain, and Ireland, and that had particularly damaging effects on the construction industries in high-wage countries such as Germany, France, or Austria.

The solution finally arrived at was a Council directive that, essentially, allows countries of destination to require all firms operating on their territory to pay at least the minimum wages generally applicable at the place of work. The directive has the effect of suspending some of the legal consequences of service liberalization—provided that the country affected is interested in, and domestically capable of,[3] taking advantage of that option. In that sense, its logic is similar to that of the 'safeguard clause' in Art. XIX of the GATT that allows

---

[3] The solution is unproblematic in countries with statutory minimum wages but creates new difficulties in countries like Germany, where collective-bargaining agreements are customarily, but without legal obligation, applied even by firms that do not belong to an employers' association.

countries to defend themselves against sectoral crises caused by free trade—an option that otherwise is not available to the member states of the European Community.

Court and Commission

Finally, there are by now also a number of cases showing that either the Commission or the European Court of Justice is beginning to limit the reach of negative integration and of European competition law, especially in the *service public* areas. In fact, the Amsterdam 'Declaration' on the status of German public banks merely took note of 'the Commission's opinion to the effect that the Community's existing competition rules allow services of general economic interest provided by public credit institutions existing in Germany'. In other words, the Commission itself had refused to intervene against the distortion of competition that allegedly follows from the fact that the operation of these public banks is secured by assets of the local and regional governments that own and use them for industrial policy purposes. Similarly, the Amsterdam 'Protocol' on public-service broadcasting was adopted against a background in which the Commission had not yet acted against publicly financed networks that were also allowed to compete for advertising revenue against their private counterparts. In both instances, therefore, the Commission itself had proceeded with caution, rather than extending competition rules to their logical conclusion. In that sense, the Amsterdam declarations and protocols were not doing much more than expressing approval and political support for the existing practice of self-restraint.

Since the Commission remains a political actor, even if its accountability is weakly institutionalized, it is perhaps to be expected that it will hesitate to apply the syllogisms of competition law regardless of the political salience of countervailing concerns. But to the great surprise of the legal profession (Reich 1994), the Court itself also seems to have done just that in the famous *Keck* decision[4] that refused to intervene, on the basis of the *Cassis* doctrine, against national rules regulating the marketing of products, rather than product quality. Similarly, after foreign transporters had gained the right of free *cabotage* through the liberalization of road haulage, the Court quite unexpectedly allowed the continuation of compulsory national tariffs, provided that they applied to foreign and domestic firms alike.[5] Finally, and most importantly in the present context, the Court also accepted the possibility that the granting of monopoly rights to the postal service and to regional suppliers of electricity (with the consequence of excluding competitors from commercially profitable services) might be acceptable if justified by a need to cross-subsidize unprofitable services in rural areas.[6] In other words, the Court itself had begun to strike a balance between the goals of competition law and the purposes served by national *service public* arrangements (Gerber 1994), well before the Amsterdam Summit explicitly requested it to do just that.

---

[4] Joined Cases 267/91 and 268/91, *Keck and Mithouard* (1993).

[5] Case 185/91, *Bundesanstalt für den Güterverkehr and Reiff* (1993). Ironically, the German Bundestag, anticipating a negative ruling of the ECJ, had unanimously repealed the tariff legislation before the case was decided (Héritier 1997).

[6] See Case 320/91P, *Procureur du Roi and Paul Courbeau* (1993), with regard to the Belgian postal monopoly, and Case 393/92, *Gemeente Almelo* v. *Energiebedijf Ijsselmij NV* (1994), with regard to the exclusive-supplier contracts of a Dutch electricity network. Both cases had come to the Court on a preliminary-opinion procedure, and both were remanded for additional factual clarification. See also Case 159/94, *Commission and France* (1997), where the Court rejected an Art. 169 action because the Commission had not fully considered the policy purposes served by the French monopolies for exporting and importing electricity and gas, and had not shown how these purposes could be achieved without restricting free trade.

There is reason to think, therefore, that, with the completion of the Internal Market programme and its extension into core areas of existing (and highly diverse) *service public* solutions of nation states, political sensitivity to the risks associated with the single-minded maximization of free market competition has increased, not only among member governments but also in the Commission. At the same time, the European Court of Justice has also begun to develop conceptual instruments that allow it to consider the relative weight that should be accorded, in light of the specific circumstances of the individual case, to the competing concerns of undistorted competition on the one hand, and the distributional, cultural, or political goals allegedly served by, say, postal monopolies, subsidized theatres, or public television on the other hand.

It is true that the Court's 'balancing test' has not yet produced explicit criteria that would provide clear guidelines to lower-court judges (Hancher 1995) or national policy makers and the Commission, for that matter (Maduro 1997). For the time being, however, that may be just as well. The 'creative ambiguity' created by the Court's dicta and the Amsterdam resolutions is likely to sensitize the zealots of undistorted competition in DG IV and elsewhere to the opportunity costs of their pursuit of legal syllogisms; at the same time, however, the ambiguity of the new rules may still appear sufficiently threatening to the protectionist proclivities of national policy makers to encourage the search for solutions that will achieve national purposes without doing so at the expense of their neighbours. In other words, what one might hope for are approximations of what I had described in an earlier article as the bipolar criteria of 'community and autonomy' (Scharpf 1994; see also Joerges 1996; Joerges and Neyer 1997). Under present conditions, so it is suggested, European integration can only proceed under rules of 'federal comity', where

European policy of negative as well as positive integration must respect the need for autonomous solutions at the national level that reflect idiosyncratic preferences, perceptions, policy traditions, and institutions. At the same time, however, national actors must respect the fact that they are members of a community of nation states that must take each others' interests and the commitment to a common venture into account when arriving at their autonomous solutions. If these complementary commitments are translated into law, the appropriate instrument can only be a balancing test whose specific implications must unfold through the case-law logic of inductive generalization from one well-considered precedent to another (Holmes 1881).

My conclusion is, therefore, that the dangers arising from the direct (legal) effect of negative integration on national problem-solving capacities are now better understood and less likely to get out of hand than could have been expected a few years ago. That, however, does not reduce the indirect (economic) effect of increased transnational mobility and regulatory and tax competition on the problem-solving capacities of the nation state. In the preceding chapter, I have discussed national policy options that might be more robust against the pressures of economic competition than existing solutions. But these will only go so far, and the interest in positive European integration remains alive among those groups and political parties that in the past have benefited from state intervention in the capitalist economy.

In the remaining sections, I will therefore discuss strategies that might increase the European capacity for problem-solving in ways that are less likely to founder on conflicts of interest or ideology among national governments in the Council. Among these, 'package deals', and 'side payments' in the form of EC structural and 'cohesion' funds, have in the past played a considerable role in obtaining the agreement of governments that would otherwise oppose certain measures (Haas 1980; Kapteyn 1991). Under the present fiscal constraints of the EU and its member states, however, these opportunities appear to be more limited, and they will be even less available under the likely conditions of eastern enlargement. I will not discuss them further here. Instead, I will explore the potential of varieties of 'differentiated integration' for facilitating European action in policy areas of high problem-solving salience and divergent national interests.

5.3 DIFFERENTIATED INTEGRATION

At least since Willy Brandt's suggestion of a two-tier or two-speed Community was taken up in the Tindemans Report (1975), the idea that positive integration could be advanced by some form of differentiation among the member states has been on the agenda of the European Community. But the notion of what criterion should be decisive for assignment to the metaphoric upper or lower echelon, to the vanguard or the rearguard, or to the core and the periphery, of European integration was always oscillating between an emphasis on the political *willingness* of countries to renounce national sovereignty and to commit themselves to closer integration on the one hand, and an emphasis on the economic *capacity* of countries to survive more intense competition or to meet more demanding standards of performance (Grabitz 1984; Giering 1997).

Since these conflicting perspectives were never resolved one way or another, the notion of differentiated integration has retained its connotation of second-class membership, even after 'opting out' from common European commitments had achieved a degree of respectability from the British and

Danish precedents. At any rate, the results of the Intergovernmental Conference leading up to the Amsterdam Summit, which had 'closer cooperation' and 'flexibility' as one of the major items on its agenda, turned out to be very disappointing. With regard to matters within the domain of the European Community (as distinguished from the second and third 'pillars' of the European Union), closer cooperation among member states is now possible within the institutions, procedures, and mechanisms of the Treaty, but its potential range is closely circumscribed by the requirements that cooperation

- must always include at least a majority of member states, and that any other member state may later join on application to the Commission;
- must be authorized by a qualified majority in the Council, and even then can be vetoed by a single government;
- must not affect Community policies, actions, or programmes; and
- must not constitute a restriction of trade or distortion of competition between member states.

If these conditions are to be respected, closer cooperation will not provide new opportunities for positive integration in policy areas where European solutions are at present blocked by fundamental conflicts among member governments. As will be recalled, at the end of Chapter 2 above I identified three types of such conflicts that may involve either

- ideological disagreement over the proper role of the state *vis-à-vis* the economy, and the proper role of the European Union *vis-à-vis* the nation state; or
- fundamental conflicts of economic self-interest arising from very large differences in the level of economic development as well as from structural differences in

the ability to profit from unrestrained competition; and
- disagreement over the content of common European policies arising from fundamental differences in existing institutional structures and policy patterns at the national level.

At the end of Chapter 3, I then showed that these conflicts have in the past blocked European solutions in a number of critical policy areas where national solutions are impeded by negative integration and the economic pressures of regulatory competition. These policy areas include

- environmental process regulations that significantly increase the cost of production of products which are exposed to international competition;
- industrial-relations regulations that are perceived as interfering with managerial prerogatives or as reducing the flexibility of labour markets;
- social-policy regulations that are perceived as raising the cost of production or increasing the reservation wages of workers; and
- the taxation of mobile factors of production, of capital incomes, and of the incomes of internationally mobile professionals.

It is not obvious that any of these issues could be dealt with more effectively under the rules and procedures of closer cooperation and flexibility as they were adopted at Amsterdam. In the sections following below, I will instead discuss a number of strategic approaches that could allow progress to be achieved on these conflict-prone issues even within the present institutional structures and procedures of the Community. I will begin with the possibility of adopting non-uniform standards for environmental process regulations.

5.3.1 Regulations at Two Levels?

Highly industrialized countries are generally affected by higher levels of environmental pollution (and contribute more to global pollution) than less developed countries. At the same time, the higher productivity of their firms, and the greater ability to pay of their consumers or taxpayers, allow the advanced countries to adopt more stringent emission standards. However, if these same standards were also applied in less developed countries, they would either destroy the competitiveness of their firms or overtax the ability to pay of consumers and taxpayers. As a consequence, agreement on regulations that would significantly increase production costs is difficult or impossible to obtain, and the European record in the field of environmental process regulations is patchy at best (Golub 1996*b*; 1996*d*; 1997*b*).

But why should that matter if countries with more serious pollution problems and a preference for more stringent regulations remain free to adopt the standards that are appropriate to their conditions? Since their higher costs are compensated by higher productivity, the threat of competition from less productive economies with lower levels of pollution control should not, in principle, deter them from doing so. What matters very much, however, is the regulatory competition among countries producing at roughly the same level of average productivity. Even if, for reasons discussed in Chapter 3, the result is not a 'race to the bottom', the threatening loss of international competitiveness has become a practically unbeatable 'killer argument' against all proposals to *raise* the level of environmental process regulations, or of 'green' taxes, by unilateral action at the national level.

The impasse might be avoided, however, by a specific variant of the idea of a 'two-tier Europe' which would allow the adoption of European regulations defining different levels of protection, rather than a single, uniform emission standard for all member states. As far as I know, this possibility has not been specifically considered in the Intergovernmental Conference. Nevertheless, its underlying logic is by no means alien to the universe of European policy options which, typically in negotiations over the entry of new members, include a considerable variety of techniques for softening or postponing the impact of the full *acquis communautaire* on countries that would face specific difficulties in adjusting.[7] Moreover, articles authorizing Community action may include specific 'safeguard clauses' allowing temporary exemptions for states that are not yet ready to shoulder the full load. A specific example is provided by Art. 130s,V TEC, which allows for temporary derogations and/or financial support from the cohesion funds if environmental policy measures should involve 'costs deemed disproportionate for the public authorities of a member state'.

However, all of these techniques maintain a pretence of universality, and they are narrowly constrained by the need to show that the differences allowed are temporary. As a consequence, countries that could not economically afford high levels of protection must try either to block European action, or to soften the impact of European regulations in the process of implementation. The price of imposing uniform rules on non-uniform economic constellations is then paid in terms of non-uniform patterns of implementation that are very difficult to control and which, if not controlled, are likely to undermine the willingness to enforce, or to obey, European rules in other countries as well. This could be changed by an explicit and general acknowledgement of differences in the state of economic development and average productivity

---

[7] Overviews of such solutions are provided by Nicoll (1984), Langeheine and Weinstock (1984), and, most comprehensively, Ehlermann (1984).

among the member states of the Community, and of the fact that these also imply differences in the ability to absorb the cost of regulations affecting production processes.

Once that premiss is accepted, the solution seems obvious: in order to facilitate the adoption of higher standards, and to eliminate the temptations of competitive deregulation,[8] there is a need for the harmonization of process-related regulations at the European level—but not necessarily for a single, uniform standard. Instead, there could be two standards, offering different levels of protection at different levels of cost.[9] Countries above a specified level of economic development could then adopt the high standards corresponding to their own needs and preferences. At the same time, less developed countries could also establish common standards at lower levels of protection and cost[10] that would still immunize them against the dangers of ruinous competition among themselves.

If that possibility did exist, one could expect that agree-

[8] It is remarkable that negative integration in the European Community includes elaborate rules to prevent distortions of competition arising from subsidies, preferential public procurement, and other forms of 'affirmative action' favouring national producers—but none against the practices of competitive deregulation and competitive tax reductions.

[9] If, instead of setting technical standards for emissions, environmental policy should rely more on 'green taxes' on energy inputs or emissions, it would be plausible to use a sliding scale, rather than two distinct levels of regulation. Thus it has been proposed that the revenue to be raised by an EC-wide environmental tax might be defined as a percentage of GDP in order to avoid disproportionate burdens on the less developed member states (von Weizsäcker 1989).

[10] It is true that the Commission's move (at British insistence) from emission standards to immissions-oriented air quality standards (Héritier et al. 1996) also reduces the regulatory cost of less polluted (i.e. less industrialized or windward) countries. However, wide-ranging or global pollution problems could not be controlled through measures defined by reference to local immissions.

ment on two-level standards will be more easily obtained than agreement on uniform European regulations that would have to be applied equally by all member states. As a consequence, European environmental policy could assume a much more active role than seems possible at present. Conversely, if the eastern enlargement of the Union is taken into view at all, progress in European regulations of production processes would come to a standstill unless differentiated standards allow the less developed countries to survive economically.

5.3.2 A Floor under Welfare Spending?

Conceivably, the logic of differentiation may also help to overcome, or at least reduce, some of the difficulties created by regulatory competition in the social policy field. As I have pointed out in Chapters 2 and 3 above, the harmonization of European welfare states is extremely difficult as a consequence of the structural and institutional heterogeneity of existing national solutions. Under these conditions, any attempt at European harmonization would require fundamental structural and institutional changes in most of the existing national systems, and we should expect fierce conflicts over which of the institutional models should be adopted at the European level. In the countries that lose out in this battle, it would be necessary to destroy, or fundamentally to reorganize, large and powerful organizations from which hundreds of thousands of employees derive their livelihood and on whose services and transfer payments large parts of the electorate have come to depend. In short, the political difficulties of harmonizing the institutional structures of mature welfare states would be so overwhelming that it is perfectly obvious why nobody, neither governments nor opposition parties, nor employers' associations nor trade unions, is at present demanding that the harmonization of social policy should be put high on the European agenda. But does that also rule out a positive European role in the reorganization of existing welfare systems which is at present on all national agendas?

As I have tried to show in Chapter 4 above, there are indeed options for a reorganization of European welfare states that could reduce mass unemployment and maintain aspirations to distributive justice even under conditions of an internationalized economy. But as I also pointed out, these solutions are difficult to design and to adopt. Under the pressures of regulatory competition and acute fiscal crises, chances are that the changes which are in fact adopted will amount to nothing more than a piecemeal dismantling of existing social benefits. As all countries are now competing to attract or retain investment capital and producing firms, all are trying to reduce the regulatory and tax burdens on capital and firms (Sinn 1993; Sinn 1994), and all are then tempted to reduce the claims of those groups—the young, the sick, the unemployed, and the old—that most depend on public services and welfare transfers.

But in the light of what was said immediately above, how could European decisions make a difference here? If there is any reason for optimism at all, it arises from the observation that, regardless of how much they differ in the patterns of social spending and in their welfare-state institutions, the member states of the European Union are remarkably alike in their revealed preferences for *total social spending* (measured as a share of GDP). By and large, the richer member states (measured by GDP per capita) have proportionately larger public social expenditures than less rich countries. This is by no means a trivial observation, since it does not hold true for the total set of industrialized OECD countries, for which there is practically no correlation between wealth and welfare spending (Fig. 5.1).

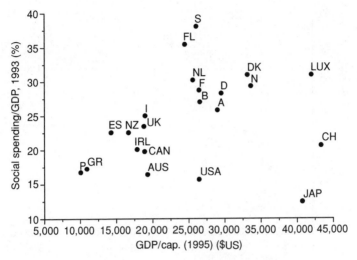

FIG. 5.1. Wealth and social spending in OECD countries

The correlation is much stronger, however, if analysis is restricted to the present members of EU 15 (Fig. 5.2),[11] and it becomes very high if the analysis (based on the latest available 1995 and 1993 data) is limited to the member states of EU 12 (thus eliminating the upper outliers Sweden and Finland which, at that time, were facing very special problems) (Fig. 5.3). By and large, the richer European countries commit proportionately larger shares of their GDP to welfare expenditures than do poorer countries. Thus, if we leave aside Sweden and Finland, past patterns of overall social spending are almost completely explained by differences in the ability to pay.

---

[11] If GDP per capita is expressed in 'purchasing power parities' rather than in US dollars at current exchange rates, the correlation is a bit lower, and some countries change positions, but the overall conclusions still hold.

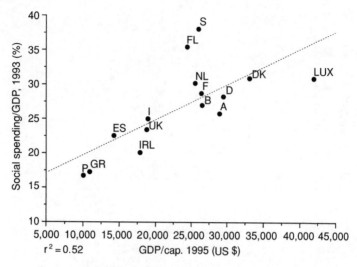

Fig. 5.2. Wealth and social spending in EU 15 member states

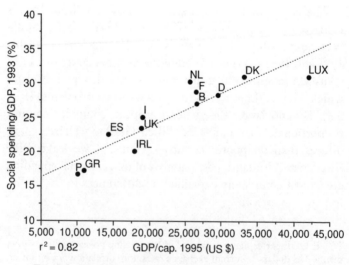

Fig. 5.3. Wealth and social spending in EU 12 member states

These figures suggest the existence of a latent consensus among the member states of the Union, according to which, regardless of structural and institutional differences, the welfare state should increase in relative importance as countries become more affluent. Beyond that, the figures also suggest the possibility that the latent consensus might be transformed into an explicit agreement among European governments according to which all countries would avoid welfare cutbacks that would push their total welfare expenditures below a lower threshold which might be defined at, or slightly below, a line connecting the locations of Portugal and Luxembourg, i.e. the lower outliers in the diagram. If such a rule were in force now, in other words, it would limit the extent to which countries could reduce overall expenditures on social transfers and services, but it would leave them free to pursue whatever structural or institutional reforms they consider necessary above that purely quantitative threshold.[12] Such an agreement would eliminate the danger (or the promise) of 'competitive welfare dismantling' from the mutual perceptions of European countries, and hence from the range of

[12] Two technical problems would require attention, however. First, since welfare spending is highly sensitive to changes in the level of unemployment, reductions of expenditure that are caused by an increase in employment should probably not be counted in defining violations of the threshold agreement. The second is that the definition of what is to be included in 'Total Social Expenditure' would require much more careful attention than was required for purposes of the OECD study on which the diagrams above are based (OECD 1996b)—this will be particularly important at the borderline between what is defined as 'public expenditure', 'mandatory private expenditure' required by statute or by collective-bargaining agreement, and 'voluntary private expenditure'. But since the agreement as well as the data base on which it depends will be the product of intergovernmental negotiations that can not succeed unless governments are interested in stipulating effective constraints, they can also make sure that the criteria by which they are willing to be judged fit the specific conditions of the countries involved.

[179]

options that could be considered in debates over welfare reforms at the national level; and it could thus help to liberate national policy choices from the tyranny of regulatory competition.[13]

5.3.3 Coordinated Institutional Reforms?

By itself, however, agreement on a lower threshold of welfare spending would be merely a holding operation that can buy time for the inevitable structural transformation of European welfare states. These transformations will have to be performed at the national level. But they could in various ways benefit from coordination at the European level. These benefits are, perhaps, more obvious for social-policy transfers and services provided by the state than they are for industrial relations at the level of the firm and the industry. In fact, however, they are important in either sector of the European welfare state.

Social Policy

Even if welfare-state reforms must be adopted at the national level, it is important for the future of social policy in Europe that the present institutional heterogeneity among national social-policy systems should be reduced. But if institutional heterogeneity at present precludes social-policy coordination, is there any reason to think that it would not also rule out convergent institutional reforms? That would indeed be likely if convergence were to be attempted as a one-step pro-

---

[13] Conceivably, a similar approach, oriented toward the share of GDP contributed to public revenue by taxes on income from capital, could also help to overcome the difficulties of European tax harmonization (Rasch 1996).

cess. The institutional status-quo positions seem too far apart to make negotiated agreement on common solutions a practical proposition. But it might nevertheless be possible to proceed in two steps. At the first stage, one might attempt to reach agreement 'in principle' on the future contours of European welfare systems that are able to assure high levels of employment together with social protection against the risks of involuntary unemployment, sickness, and poverty, under conditions of demographic change, changing family structures, changing employment patterns, and intensified economic competition. In fact, as contributions to the OECD High-Level Conference 'Beyond 2000: The New Social Policy Agenda' have shown, these contours are already visible. Proposals from quite diverse quarters seem to converge on a combination of employment-intensive forms of tax-financed basic income support with health insurance systems and (funded) pension schemes that will be financed through individual contributions, part of which will be mandated by law, and subsidized for low-income groups (Bovenberg and van der Linden 1997; Esping-Andersen 1997; Haveman 1997). In fact, proposals of this nature, even if they represent radical departures from the status quo, seem to be surprisingly uncontroversial—provided that discussion focuses on the abstract desirability and effectiveness of solutions within a longer-term perspective (OECD 1997*b*).

The difficulties of agreement would, of course, be immensely greater if it should come to the second step of designing ways for getting from here to there—from the divergent status-quo conditions and political constraints of individual countries to a functionally superior and more convergent model of the future European welfare state (Esping-Andersen 1996). But here, the Community might take advantage of the fact that structural and institutional heterogeneity, while extremely great across all member states, is not universal. As

Harold Wilensky, Peter Flora, Gøsta Esping-Andersen, and others have shown, European welfare states can be grouped into institutional 'families' that share specific historical roots, basic value orientations, solution concepts, and administrative practices, and whose path-dependent evolution has required them to cope with similar difficulties in comparable ways.[14] Without going into any more detail here, within the present European Union it is possible to identify at least four such 'families':

- Scandinavian welfare states which are mainly financed from general tax revenue and which emphasize generous income replacement together with universally available and high-quality public services, including public health care;
- Continental systems with relatively generous income-maintaining social transfers and health care financed primarily from employment-based social insurance contributions, and with a relatively low commitment to social services;
- southern systems which represent less comprehensive and less generous versions of the Continental model; and
- the British-Irish system which emphasizes egalitarian and tax-financed basic pensions, unemployment benefits, and health services, while leaving other forms of income replacement and services to private initiative and the family.

These grouping are certainly not clearly separated from each other. In the Netherlands, for instance, there are elements of the Continental and the Scandinavian models combined, and

---

[14] See e.g. Wilensky (1975); Alber (1982); Flora (1986); Esping-Andersen (1990); Alber and Bernardi-Schenkluhn (1991); Castles and Mitchel (1993); J. Schmid (1996).

while Italy corresponds most to the Continental model, its health care system was reformed along British lines in the 1970s and it also shares some of the characteristics of the southern model (Alber and Bernardi-Schenkluhn 1991). Nevertheless, there is reason to think that among the present members of the Union, there are relatively distinct groups of countries that share important aspects of their welfare-state structures and institutions, that are likely to face similar problems, and that will therefore benefit not only from examining each others' experiences, but also from coordinating their reform strategies. If these discussions are managed and monitored by the Commission, it should at least be possible to initiate moves towards greater institutional convergence over the longer term.

Industrial Relations

Coordinated approaches would be equally valuable for the reform of industrial-relations systems, where institutional differences seem to be even more important than in public- or state-sponsored social-policy areas (Crouch 1993). At present, pressures for reform are felt most acutely in Scandinavian and Continental systems characterized by corporatist arrangements at the sectoral and national level and codetermination at the level of the firm. Since they are most highly institutionalized, they are seen to suffer from severe competitive disadvantages in comparison to the flexibility of purely market-driven Anglo–American systems. Nevertheless, corporatism and cooperative industrial relations have in the past benefited considerably from their capacity to control wage inflation and to raise industrial productivity (Scharpf 1991; Streeck 1992; Garrett 1998). These advantages are likely to be destroyed as each country responds individually to present pressures for labour-market

[183]

flexibility and unfettered managerial prerogatives (Streeck 1995*b*; 1997*a*).

Given the institutional heterogeneity of national systems, there is certainly no chance for creating a universal European industrial-relations regime that would institutionalize sectoral corporatism in all member states or codetermination in the corporate structures of the *Societas Europea* (Streeck 1997*b*). Yet it seems obvious that if reforms could be coordinated among the group of corporatist countries,[15] there would be a much better chance of defining and adopting path-dependent institutional changes that would increase flexibility while still preserving the advantages that coopera-tive corporatism had enjoyed in the past.

There is reason to think, however, that a still heavier burden of adjustment must be faced by European industrial-relations systems that are neither corporatist nor purely mar-ket-driven. They seem to be at a competitive disadvantage against both countries with more flexible labour markets and countries with more disciplined and cooperative unions, and they probably will need to move one way or another, toward the Austrian or the British model, in order to increase their competitiveness and their attractiveness to internationally mobile capital investments. Again, it seems likely that the need for adjustment and the options available could be clari-fied, and the adoption of reforms facilitated, by coordinated approaches among countries that find themselves confronted with similar problems.

[15] One characteristic disadvantage of corporatist systems is their seem-ing complexity and lack of transparency for foreign investors, which is greatly increased by the variety of idiosyncratic national corporatisms. At a time when the importance of foreign direct investment increases, therefore, coordination could by itself increase the attractiveness of all corporatist systems.

Needed: Opportunities for Sub-European Coordination

If the Amsterdam decisions on 'closer cooperation and flexibility' had allowed for the formation of groupings that comprise less than half of all member states, it might have been most promising to use the institutional infrastructure of the Community, and especially the analytical and coordinative services of the Commission, to assist the development of social-policy and industrial-relations reforms which are suited to the specific conditions of groups of countries and, at the same time, would represent convergent moves toward the common longer-term perspective of European welfare states. That would have been a most effective arrangement for counteracting any tendencies toward 'competitive welfare dismantling'. Moreover, and even more important, in the domestic politics of each of the participating countries, the reform of existing welfare systems could have benefited, against ubiquitous opposition, from the legitimacy bonus of internationally coordinated solutions, and perhaps even from the legal force of EC directives.

Under the circumstances, however, the institutional infrastructure that would most facilitate coordination is not in place. The heterogeneity of existing national structures and institutions, and of the specific problems they must face, is far too great to allow the development of uniform reform strategies; at the same time, purely national reform efforts are operating under constraints of international regulatory competition that are likely to favour suboptimal solutions to be adopted by unilateral reform. Under these conditions, it is nevertheless important to point out that coordinated reform strategies among countries that share critical institutional preconditions are more promising, in principle, than unilateral coping strategies at the national level.

[185]

There is a need, therefore, for institutional arrangements that allow countries sharing similar problems to coordinate their reform strategies. Conceivably, some of these benefits could also be achieved through Schengen-type arrangements outside the institutional framework of the Community—but that would not only lose the organizational support of the Commission but would also presuppose a greater degree of prior consensus among the participating governments than could be expected before the beginning of the analytical and conceptual work that must be done to identify common solutions. But perhaps, as was in the end true of Schengen, if 'closer cooperation' is initiated by some countries outside the Community framework, then the next Intergovernmental Conference will again find a way of incorporating such arrangements in the constitution of the European Union.

Conclusion: Multi-level Problem-Solving in Europe

If we now return to the questions raised in the opening chapter, what have we learned about democratic legitimacy in the multi-level European polity?

There is, first, no reason to revise the sceptical view on input-oriented legitimacy at the European level. None of the arguments that could be advanced in its support (e.g. Weiler 1995; 1997a; 1997b; Habermas 1996) is able to overcome the triple deficits of the lack of a pre-existing sense of collective identity, the lack of Europe-wide policy discourses, and the lack of a Europe-wide institutional infrastructure that could assure the political accountability of office holders to a European constituency. Though some of these deficits might have been reduced through feasible, or at least not a-priori impossible, institutional reforms—e.g. by having the President of the Commission elected by, and fully accountable to, the European Parliament—the overall perspective has significantly deteriorated after the decision of the Amsterdam Summit to go ahead with negotiations over the eastern enlargement of the Union without first agreeing on even the minimally necessary constitutional reforms. With the entry of Central and Eastern European member states, the economic, institutional, cultural, and linguistic heterogeneity of the nations comprising the Union will increase again. By the same token, prospects of a European collective identity, and of Europe-wide political discourses that could legitimize majority decisions on politically salient issues, will recede even further into a dimly perceived future. The implication is that, for the time being and for all currently practical purposes, the European polity will lack the quality of *government by the people*, and that all discourses that attempt to draw on input-oriented legitimizing arguments can only exacerbate the perception of an irremediable European democratic deficit. As a consequence, moves toward majority decisions in the Council, and toward reducing the size of the Commission, will become even more difficult as concerns about the dangers of being outvoted are now rising even among those governments that in the past argued for decision rules approximating majoritarian democracy.

However, as I have tried to show in Chapter 1, even in constitutional democracies at the national level, input-oriented arguments could never carry the full burden of legitimizing the exercise of governing power. They are everywhere supplemented, and in many policy areas (e.g. in monetary policy, or in the wide range of issues left to judicial law-making) displaced, by output-oriented arguments showing how specific institutional arrangements are conducive to *government for the people*—meaning that they will favour policy choices that can be justified in terms of consensual notions of the public interest. In the classical (or Kantian) terminology, these arguments are part of *republican*, rather than *democratic*, legitimizing discourses; in the language of democratic self-determination, what matters is the institutional capacity for effective problem-solving, and the presence of institutional safeguards against the abuse of public power. In principle, at any rate, there is no reason why governance at the European level should not also be supported by output-oriented legitimacy arguments.

If there are doubts on that score, these are, by and large, not caused by major concerns about the abuse of European public power. Even though the political accountability of the

Commission and its President appears quite weak when compared with that of a parliamentary government, the dependence of positive Commission action either on the support of member state governments in the Council or on approval by the European Court of Justice seems sufficiently strong to render deliberate wrongdoing a lesser concern. What is more doubtful, by contrast, is the European capacity for effective problem-solving. In that regard, however, there are significant differences between different areas of European policy-making.

Beginning with the distinction between negative and positive integration (which is related to, but not congruent with, the distinction between market-making and market-correcting policy interventions), I have tried to show, in Chapter 2, how the Commission and the Court have been able to develop the former into an extremely powerful set of legal tools for removing national barriers to the free movement of goods, services, capital, and workers within the Community, and for intervening against national policies that could be construed as distortions of free market competition. The legitimization of these policies rests formally on the primary law of the Treaties that were adopted by the governments and ratified by the parliaments of all member states. But these tools of negative integration have also been used to achieve the liberalization and, in effect, privatization of a wide range of service and infrastructure functions which, in all member states, had been exempted from market competition at the time when the Treaties were concluded and for many decades thereafter. Hence the substantive legitimization of European policies requiring the liberalization of *service public* functions rests on the authority of European and national legal systems and their capacities for judicial law-making that are not under the control of democratically accountable governments and parliaments. Their acceptance rests, in other words, on legitimizing beliefs that place trust in the internal control mechanisms within the legal system, and in the validation of judicial law-making through specialized discourses within the legal profession that are, it is hoped, anchored in broadly held notions of public interest and justice.

By contrast, positive integration and market-correcting interventions at the European level are only to a very limited extent able to rely on the law-making capacities of the Commission and the Court acting on their own. Instead, they depend on agreement among national governments in the Council of Ministers and, increasingly, on the agreement of the European Parliament. Under these conditions, I have argued, the output-oriented legitimacy of European policy choices that are in fact able to cross these very high hurdles of negotiated agreement is not really in doubt. Compared to national decision processes, there is a wider range of interests that has access to, and must be considered in, European policy processes, and the fact that majority voting is not generally available to close out opposing arguments makes it more likely that the solutions actually adopted will represent genuine efforts to reach the Pareto frontier. Moreover, the active role of the supranational Commission, the good services of 'Europeanized' civil servants in COREPER, and the socialization of national representatives into the 'deliberative' search for consensual solutions in 'comitology' discussions (Joerges and Neyer 1997) all combine to increase the likelihood that potential 'win-win' solutions will in fact be discovered and eventually adopted in positive-integration processes as well.

But even if all that is claimed for the 'supranational' effectiveness of European institutions were true (and I have overstated their potential in the paragraph above), there remains the stark 'intergovernmental' fact that the agreement of national governments in the Council is necessary for major decisions of positive integration, and that these governments not only have powerful incentives, but are duty-bound and opposition-pressed to represent what they and their constituents consider to be important national interests in European negotiations. Hence there are definite limits to the possibilities of a 'deliberative' redefinition of government preferences. That also implies that there will be ranges of potential policy choices on the European level that are ruled out because effective solutions are located outside the negotiation space that is defined, for all member governments, by their 'best alternative to negotiated agreement' (Scharpf 1997a: ch. 6).

As a consequence, it should not come as a surprise that in the areas of positive integration researchers focusing on different policy areas should have come to widely differing conclusions with regard to the problem-solving capacity of European decision processes. As I have tried to show in Chapter 3 above, these differences can generally be explained by the underlying constellations of national interests as they are represented in the specialized sessions of the Council of Ministers. Where these interests converge or are complementary, European policy processes (because of their greater specialization, and because of the agenda-setting role of the Commission) may even pursue and achieve more ambitious goals than would be possible within the more activist nation states. This is most likely to be true with regard to regulations of product quality where in the absence of common European rules the economic advantages of the larger European market could not be realized, but similar conditions have been shown to exist in some other policy areas as well (Eichener 1997; Joerges and Neyer 1997; Pollack 1997a; Scharpf 1997c; Vogel 1997).

By contrast, the European capacity for positive integration is systematically constrained in those areas where national interests diverge and where, in the absence of legitimate majority decisions, opposition cannot simply be overruled. This, I have tried to show in Chapter 2 and 3, is most likely to be the case with regard to market-correcting regulations that would add to the cost of economic production without providing direct benefits to individual consumers, or that would reduce the post-tax rate of return on capital investments—i.e. in the fields of environmental process regulations, of social-policy and industrial-relations legislation, and of redistributive taxation. In these fields, conflicts of interest between governments representing countries with advanced and less advanced economies and with divergent policy traditions and institutional structures are likely to make agreement on common European rules difficult or impossible.

Nor is this simply a question of decision rules at the European level. Market-correcting regulations can succeed only as parts of a complex configuration of rules and practices which must maintain and increase allocative efficiency and competitiveness at the same time as they are protecting the non-economic values of a society. Hence, as the growing literature on 'varieties of capitalism' is demonstrating (Albert 1993; Berger and Dore 1996; Crouch and Streeck 1997; Hollingsworth and Boyer 1997), post-war political economies have differed greatly not only in the *extent* to which the capitalist economy was embedded in (i.e. constrained and supported by) societal institutions, but also in the *characteristic ways* in which this embeddedness was institutionalized in Japan and in the capitalist welfare states on the European continent (Streeck 1998). There is, in other words, not a single type of non-Anglo-Saxon 'welfare capitalism', or a single 'European social model', which could be adopted for the European Community if only the votes were available in the Council of Ministers. Instead, there are diverse, historically contingent, and complex national solutions, deeply embedded in the institutions, values, and established practices of specific societies—constantly evolving and changing, it is true, but capable of changing only in path-dependent ways if change is to be distinguished from dismantling. In fact, the only solution that could be uniformly imposed would be the Anglo-American form of deregulated and disembedded capitalism, but not a common model of (reconstructed) embeddedness.

In other words, European-level policy is at its strongest in the field of negative integration where the Commission and the Court have been politically unconstrained in expanding the range and intensity of market competition, and it is at its weakest in those areas where existing market-correcting regulations at the national level are most directly challenged by more intense economic competition. In that sense, it is indeed true that European integration has greatly reduced the range of national policy options for the governing of capitalist economies without being able to recreate a commensurate governing capacity at the European level (Streeck 1995*a*).

However, as I have tried to show in Chapter 4, a reduced range of policy options does not imply that there will be no significant policy choices left at the national level. Being prevented by negative integration from protecting national producers against foreign competitors, or from obstructing the relocation of firms and the outflow of capital, European nation states cannot avoid the 'competition among regulatory systems'. It does not follow, however, that this competition must necessarily result in convergence on the 'lowest common denominator' of Anglo-American forms of deregulated capitalism.

To the extent that they have not done so before, it is indeed necessary that national political economies must learn to compete in an environment in which national boundary controls have been eliminated within Europe, and have lost much of

[193]

their effectiveness in the world beyond the European Union. But competitiveness can be achieved in a great variety of ways. Head-on competition on the factor costs of mass-produced consumer goods is only one of these—and certainly not the most promising one in light of the much greater cost advantages of South-East Asian and Eastern European competitors. Even when engaging in price competition, countries could choose between strategies that emphasize the reduction of wage costs, regulatory costs, and taxation, and strategies exploiting the productivity gains that can be achieved through a better-trained workforce, more cooperative industrial relations, and the more effective use of advanced production methods. More importantly, however, the opening of European and world markets not only increases the number of potential competitors, but also creates more attractive opportunities for specialization. To the extent that firms are able to concentrate on the specific needs of buyers in particular market niches, they may gain competitive advantages that are relatively robust against the pressures of price competition (Soskice 1990). The outcome could again be a form of ecological equilibrium in which intense competition will not result in a universal race to the bottom but, rather, in relatively stable patterns of a new international division of labour in which national economies with very different production profiles and cost structures will coexist in complex interdependence.

For the territorial state that must try to maintain production and employment within its own boundaries, the implication is that there will still be significant choices among alternative industrial strategies. Cost-cutting and deregulation is only one of them, and may not be the most attractive one for high-cost countries. Building upon the strength of existing production profiles by providing the infrastructure support at the national level (and, increasingly, at regional and local levels) that will allow firms to exploit the advantages of specialization may be at the same time more effective and less destructive of the non-economic values that had been served by the European variants of embedded capitalism.

In any case, however, more intense competition in international markets will increase demands on the skills and flexibility of workers in the exposed sectors of high-cost economies. Hence national attempts to maintain high levels of employment for all job seekers must also include strategies facilitating the expansion of a sheltered sector in which goods and services are locally produced for local consumption. As I have shown in Chapter 4, advanced industrial economies differ greatly in the size of this sheltered sector, and Continental European welfare states are particularly weak in this regard. The explanation is found in the peculiar structure of welfare states that raise reservation wages through relatively generous social transfers while relying primarily on payroll taxes for their source of finance. If that explanation is accepted, however, it is also clear that solutions facilitating the expansion of service employment in the sheltered sector will depend on modifications in the design of these welfare systems.

That solution points to a more general maxim that should guide the adjustment strategies of welfare states under conditions of regulatory competition. As the data presented in Chapter 4 demonstrate, the size of the welfare state as such is not inimical to high employment, either overall or even in the sectors that are exposed to international competition. What matters very much, however, is specific features in the design of national welfare states that may be more or less compatible with, or vulnerable to, international regulatory competition. What is needed, therefore, in those member states of the European Union that are politically committed to maintaining social protection and equality above the levels provided by the Anglo-American models, is a systematic search for more robust solutions that can be maintained even in the face of international mobility and more intensive competition. From what has been said, it follows that these should be solutions which, *ceteris paribus*, will increase rather than reduce private-sector employment; which will not further increase the costs of production; and which do not primarily depend on the revenue from mobile tax bases. Which specific solutions would meet these abstract criteria, and would, at the same time, be institutionally and politically feasible under the conditions prevailing in a particular country and at a particular time, can of course not be specified at the same level of abstraction. What matters here is the direction of the search that could lead to such solutions, and the claim that some countries are in fact successful in that search (Visser and Hemerijck 1997).

In order to succeed, however, these countries must find a way to maintain democratic legitimacy even if new policy solutions must necessarily violate vested interests and disappoint long-held expectations. Moreover, in countries with fragmented political institutions and multiple veto points, successful strategy change depends on a convergence of cognitive and normative orientations among a plurality of (semi-) independent actors that is difficult to achieve even under the best of circumstances. What is needed, in other words, is a common understanding of the country's future place in a competitive economic environment, of the functional and policy requirements for attaining and holding that place, and of the 'new architecture of legitimate inequalities' (Streeck 1998) that will go together with the competitive strategy that is being adopted. Even though the magnitude of the required changes will differ from one country to another (V. Schmidt 1997), the protected European welfare states of the early post-war decades must indeed transform themselves into 'competitive welfare states' if they are to survive beyond the end of the century.

At minimum that will require public discourses that review the way of raising welfare revenue so as to minimize the impact on the cost of production, and that also review the structure of welfare benefits so as to increase opportunities and incentives to work, rather than the attractiveness of paid non-work (Phelps 1997). But then, as they learn to compete in order to survive, European welfare states must also learn to compete in ways that acknowledge their interdependence, their common vulnerability, and their common commitment to the values of social integration and solidarity. Even though they cannot realize these values through uniform policies adopted at the European level, they must pursue their national solutions in ways that are compatible with their European obligations, and that reflect their membership in a community that is committed to restraining the use of strategies which, if pursued by all, could only harm everyone. In other words, a European constellation of 'competitive welfare states' would degenerate into a race to the bottom unless its constituent members are constrained from competing through 'beggar-my-neighbour' strategies.

That may sound like a moral double bind—to compete and to avoid effective competition at the same time. But that objection is no more valid here than it would be for a rule against doping in competitive sports. Instead, the problem arises from the dilemma-character of moral injunctions that are based on the Kantian categorical imperative. Even if everyone would agree that universal doping is unacceptable, the temptation of winning could be too strong to make the rule self-enforcing, especially if the definition of impermissible practices was not very precise to begin with; and if some were suspected of winning by illicit means, others might feel compelled to follow suit in order to stay in the game. What are obviously needed under such conditions are the defining, monitoring, and enforcement functions of an impartial agency that is charged with applying the rule.

Fortunately for Europe, the Commission and the European Court of Justice are available to perform precisely these functions. It may be true that the distinction between the legitimate 'competition among regulatory systems' and the 'ruinous competition' of beggar-my-neighbour policies is even less clear than the line between legitimate food additives and doping is in the world of sport. There are indeed no hard and fast rules. Assuming that political agreement on a lower boundary for welfare spending (discussed in Chapter 5) cannot be reached, the Court could not intervene against countries that have decided to reduce the overall size of their welfare state, or to move from welfare to 'workfare', or from payroll taxes to the value-added tax in financing welfare expenditures. But it still would be possible to intervene against competitive tax concessions, competitive forms of deregulation, and similar practices. The criterion in every case would be Kantian: given the preferences of the adopting country, would measures of this kind become self-defeating if they were simultaneously adopted by all other countries? This may appear as an overly abstract test, but the distinctions required here are hardly more difficult than the line that the Commission and the Court are already asked to draw between allowable and impermissible state subsidies (Arts. 92–4 TEC), or between valid or invalid regulations that have the effect of non-tariff barriers but are allegedly justified by concerns for the health and safety of marketable products (Art. 36 TEC).

At another level, what is required here is no more difficult than the task the law must face when regulating the competition among private economic agents. National competition law necessarily includes both rules against impediments to 'free competition' and rules against excessive or 'unfair competition'. Since it was not possible, at least initially, to define hard and fast rules balancing the equally valid requirements of free and fair competition, the effective regulation of competition did in fact evolve through case law more than through legislation. By the same token, it would be difficult to define precise rules of general application that would clearly distinguish between legitimate and 'unfair' forms of competition between systems of national regulation and taxation.

But if rules must, in any case, be developed in light of the specific facts of concrete cases, it seems highly pertinent to ask who would be better able to decide these cases, the representatives of national governments in the Council of Ministers or the Commission and the Court in legal proceedings? When the issue of a 'code of conduct' on the competitive manipulation of business taxes was finally confronted by the Council of Economic and Finance Ministers in December of 1997, the prevailing view was that the formulation and application of such rules should be strictly understood as a 'political commitment' that would not affect the 'rights and obligations . . . of the Member States . . . in accordance with the Treaty' (ECOFIN 1997). In other words, the intention was that the European Court could not be called upon to sanction breaches of this sort of political commitment.

But that may not be the most effective solution. It is true that having national tax policies laid open, discussed, and criticized in the Council would be an improvement, and some ministers would indeed find themselves in a difficult spot having to justify to their peers glaring departures from commonly acceptable standards. Nevertheless, discussions in ECOFIN will not conform to the ideal of 'deliberative' decision-making, and the finance minister who is being grilled in Brussels may not be free to change tax rules that were hammered out in complex political compromises at

[199]

home. Since colleagues may anticipate similar difficulties of their own, agreement on any 'political' sanctions will be difficult to reach.

In light of the specific character of the issues involved, it seems thus worth exploring whether the approach that has successfully advanced negative integration in the European Community would not be more effective and more appropriate here as well. There, member governments had agreed on the desirability of market integration, but being aware of their own inclinations toward protectionist practices, and of the complexities of the issues involved, they decided to delegate the enforcement to the supranational Commission, and to leave the elaboration of rules to the case law of judicial decisions, guided by the parallel evolution of a discourse on European competition law in the transnational legal profession.

Similarly, we now seem to have an emergent consensus on the desirability of some limits on intra-European regulatory and tax competition, combined with an awareness of the temptations that would prevent this agreement from being self-enforcing. Moreover, there is now a greater awareness of the lasting limitations of European political integration. People have come to realize that the European Union will not, in the foreseeable future, become a democratic polity, and that even if the European Parliament should be further strengthened, it would not be legitimate to resort to majority decisions in order to overrule the strong resistance of some countries. At the same time, it should also have become obvious that the heterogeneity of national economic interests and institution-based preferences will make agreement in the Council of Ministers difficult or impossible in those policy areas where the welfare state is most challenged by the economic competition among national regulatory systems.

Under these circumstances, it makes sense to think about

complementing *political* efforts to advance positive integration by parallel efforts to expand the problem-solving potential of *legal integration*. Europe, after all, has advanced much further as a legal order than as a political system (Weiler 1982; Burley and Mattli 1993; Mestmäcker 1994; Joerges 1994*a*; 1996). As was pointed out in Chapter 2 above, it is true that the law-making potential of European legal processes has so far mainly served the advancement of negative integration. But that is not so by logical necessity, and there is no constitutional reason why the practical thrust of European law should be limited to the market-making imperatives of liberalization and deregulation. At the national level, at any rate, judicial activism has contributed as much to the expansion of social rights as it did to the protection of economic freedoms, and the same has been true in European Community law within the limited field of gender discrimination.

If member states were indeed interested in protecting themselves against the temptations of 'unfair competition', the development of a European case law regulating the competition among regulatory systems would probably require some explicit legitimization in the primary law of the Treaties. But that mandate need be no more concrete than the provisions authorizing the Commission to control national subsidies (Arts. 92–4 TEC). Moreover, if judicial protection could be extended to the individual rights already postulated—in the form of a declaration of the heads of state or government—in the 'Social Charter' of 1989 (European Commission 1990), European and national courts could also develop very powerful instruments for constraining any temptation of 'social dumping'.

Beyond that, it would be for the legal profession to discuss and define justiciable criteria, and to explore the procedural conditions under which parties might have standing to raise issues of unfair regulatory competition in 'cases and controversies' before national courts and in proceedings before the European Court of Justice, and it would be for the Commission to develop and select appropriate cases to test the scope of its own power. In other words, what one should then expect is the further exploration and colonization of new territory by the standard processes through which the boundaries of European law have been steadily extended ever since the landmark decisions of the early 1960s.

Of course, even if regime competition should be legally moderated among the members of the European Union, that would still provide no protection against competitors from outside. However, since the Union as a whole is much less dependent on foreign trade than is true of each of its members, the problem is much less severe to begin with. Moreover, in its relations with the outside world, the European Commission has in the past been quite ready to use 'voluntary' restraint agreements and the anti-dumping options available under the GATT and WTO Treaties in ways which it would never have allowed member states to use against each other. There is thus no reason to think that these instruments would not also be employed to provide protection for the 'European social model' against some of the pressures of global economic competition. In other words, a regime of 'embedded liberalism', while no longer feasible on the national level, is still viable as an option on the European level.

So where does that leave us in our concern about democratic legitimacy in the multi-level European polity? The main challenges, it should have become clear, must be faced at the national level where European welfare states must find solutions that are compatible with, and robust against, much more intense international economic competition. This transformation of formerly protected into competitive welfare states is difficult to achieve in any case, and to achieve it without endangering democratic legitimacy is a task that will severely tax the integrative capabilities of political elites in all countries.

European policy, by contrast, is much less under challenge. As shown in Chapter 3 above, its effectiveness is limited to certain policy areas of relatively low political salience in which its legitimacy is not really in doubt. To move beyond these fields would require a fundamental transformation of the Union into a common political space for which all important preconditions are still lacking. At the same time, however, Europe has become the economic space within which producers and consumers are orienting their choices, and it is in the process of becoming the sociocultural space that students and teachers, artists and audiences, and of course millions of tourists take for granted in their search for enlightenment, information, pleasure, and excitement. As this is happening, Europe is also becoming the legal space within which economic actors as well as citizens can freely and confidently move and transact among each other.

To make all this possible, it was necessary for the member states of the Union to transfer certain competencies to the supranational level, and to pool their sovereignties in other policy areas. More important for present purposes: even in those important fields where responsibility for public policy must, for the foreseeable future, remain at the national level, the traditional patterns of international relations among sovereign nation states are being transformed into reflexive interactions among the members of a community of states that are aware of their interdependence, their common vulnerability, and their obligation to consider the impact on others as they are trying to deal with their own problems (Joerges 1997). If this is fully recognized, and translated into rules of European law under the guardianship of the Commission and the Court, the 'competition among regulatory systems' can be contained in ways that no longer threaten the democratic legitimacy of national polities. Thus, by assuring the reflexivity of national policy choices, European law will in fact safeguard the democratic legitimacy of the multi-level polity that Europe has become and must be.

REFERENCES

ACKERMAN, BRUCE A. (1992), *The Future of Liberal Revolution*. New Haven: Yale University Press.

AKERLOF, GEORGE (1971), 'The Market for "Lemons": Quality Uncertainty and the Market Mechanism', *Quarterly Journal of Economics*, 84: 488–500.

ALBER, JENS (1982), *Vom Armenhaus zum Wohlfahrtsstaat: Analysen zur Entwicklung der Sozialversicherung in Westeuropa*. Frankfurt am Main: Campus.

——BERNARDI-SCHENKLUHN, BRIGITTE (1991), *Westeuropäische Gesundheitssysteme im Vergleich*. Frankfurt am Main: Campus.

ALBERT, MICHEL (1993), *Capitalism vs. Capitalism*. London: Whurr.

ALTER, KAREN J. (1996), 'The European Court's Political Power', *West European Politics*, 19: 458–87.

BACHRACH, PETER, and BARATZ, MORTON S. (1970), *Power and Poverty: Theory and Practice*. New York: Oxford University Press.

BAKHOVEN, ANTON F. (1990), 'An Alternative Assessment of the Macro-economic Effects of "Europe 1992"', in Horst Siebert (ed.), *The Completion of the Internal Market: Symposium 1989*. Tübingen: Mohr, 24–52.

BASEDOW, JÜRGEN (1992), *Von der deutschen zur europäischen Wirtschaftsverfassung*. Walter Eucken Institut. Vorträge und Aufsätze 137. Tübingen: Mohr.

BEHRENS, PETER (1994), 'Die Wirtschaftsverfassung der Europäischen Gemeinschaft', in Gert Brüggemeier (ed.), *Verfassungen für ein ziviles Europa*. Baden-Baden: Nomos, 73–90.

BENZ, ARTHUR, and LEHMBRUCH, GERHARD (1996), 'Demokratische Legitimation regionaler Politik im europäischen Mehrebenensystem', MS. Halle: Institut für Politikwissenschaft, Universität Halle-Wittenberg.

BERGER, SUZANNE, and DORE, RONALD (eds.) (1996), *National Diversity and Global Capitalism*. Ithaca, NY: Cornell University Press.

BICKEL, ALEXANDER M. (1962), *The Least Dangerous Branch: The Supreme Court at the Bar of Politics*. Indianapolis: Bobbs Merrill.

BLANCHARD, OLIVIER (1997), 'Is There a Core of Usable Macroeconomics?', *American Economic Review*, 87 (2): 244–6.

BMA (1995), *Euro-Atlas: Soziale Sicherheit im Vergleich*. Bonn: Bundesministerium für Arbeit und Sozialordnung.

——(1996), *Euro-Atlas: Soziale Sicherheit im Vergleich*. Bonn: Bundesministerium für Arbeit und Sozialordnung.

BOVENBERG, A. L., and LINDEN, A. S. M. VAN DER (1997), 'Can We Afford to Grow Old?' Paper presented at the OECD High Level Conference 'Beyond 2000: The New Social Policy Agenda'. Paris, 12–13 Nov.

BRENNAN, GEOFFREY, and BUCHANAN, JAMES M. (1985), *The Reason of Rules: Constitutional Political Economy*. Cambridge: Cambridge University Press.

BURLEY, ANNE-MARIE, and MATTLI, WALTER (1993), 'Europe before the Court: A Political Theory of Legal Integration', *International Organization*, 47: 41–76.

CANOVA, TIMOTHY A. (1994), 'The Swedish Model Betrayed', *Challenge*, 37 (3): 36–40.

CARUSO, DANIELA (1997), 'The Missing View of the Cathedral: The Private Law Paradigm of European Legal Interpretation', *European Law Journal*, 3: 3–32.

CARY, WILLIAM L. (1974), 'Federalism and Corporate Law: Reflections on Delaware', *Yale Law Journal*, 83: 663–705.

CASTLES, FRANCIS G., and MITCHEL, DEBORAH (1993), 'Worlds of Welfare and Families of Nations', in Francis G. Castles (ed.), *Families of Nations: Patterns of Public Policy in Western Democracies*. Aldershot: Elgar, 93–128.

CERNY, PHILIP G. (1994), 'The Dynamics of Financial Globalization: Technology, Market Structure, and Policy Response', *Policy Sciences*, 27: 319–42.

COASE, RONALD H. (1996), 'The Problem of Social Cost', *Journal of Law and Economics*, 3: 1–44.

COEN, DAVID (1997), 'The Evolution of the Large Firm as a Political Actor in the European Union', *Journal of European Public Policy*, 4: 91–108.

COHEN, JOSHUA (1989), 'Deliberation and Democratic Legitimacy', in Alan Hamlin and Philip Pettit (eds.), *The Good Polity: Normative Analysis of the State.* Oxford: Blackwell, 17–34.

——and ROGERS, JOEL (1993), 'Secondary Associations and Democratic Governance', *Politics and Society*, 20: 393–472.

————(1993), 'Associations and Democracy', *Social Philosophy and Policy*, 10: 282–312.

——and SABEL, CHARLES (1997), 'Directly-Deliberative Polyarchy', *European Law Journal*, 3: 313–42.

COLOMER, JOSEP M. (1996), 'Introduction', in Josep M. Colomer (ed.), *Political Institutions in Europe.* London: Routledge, 1–17.

COURCHENE, THOMAS J. (1983), 'Analytical Perspectives on the Canadian Economic Union', in Michael J. Trebilcock, J. Robert S. Prichard, Thomas J. Courchene, and John Whalley (eds.), *Federalism and the Canadian Economic Union.* Toronto: University of Toronto Press, 51–110.

COX, HELMUT (1996), 'Öffentliche Dienstleistungen und europäische Wettbewerbsordnung: Das europäische Gemeinschaftsrecht unter dem Einfluß des Service Public-Gedankens', *Hamburger Jahrbuch für Wirtschafts- und Gesellschaftspolitik*, 41. Tübingen: Mohr, 161–88.

CROUCH, COLIN (1993), *Industrial Relations and European State Traditions.* Oxford: Clarendon.

——and STREECK, WOLFGANG (eds.) (1997), *Political Economy of Modern Capitalism: Mapping Convergence & Diversity.* London: Sage.

CROZIER, MICHEL, HUNTINGTON, SAMUEL P., and WATANUKI, JOJI (1975), *The Crisis of Democracy: Report on the Governability of Democracies to the Trilateral Commission.* New York: New York University Press.

DEHOUSSE, RENAUD (1995), 'Constitutional Reform in the European Community: Are there Alternatives to the Majority Avenue?', *West European Politics*, 18: 118–36.

——and WEILER, JOSEPH H. H. (1990), 'The Legal Dimension', in William Wallace (ed.), *The Dynamics of European Integration.* London: Pinter, 242–60.

DIW (1996), 'Auswirkungen der Einführung eines Bürgergeldes: Neue Berechnungen des DIW', *DIW Wochenbericht*, 27/1996.

DRYZEK, JOHN S. (1990), *Discursive Democracy: Politics, Policy, and Political Science*. Cambridge: Cambridge University Press.

ECOFIN (1997), 'Resolution of the Council and the Representatives of the Governments of the Member States, Meeting within the Council of 1 December 1997 on a Code of Conduct for Business Taxation', *Official Journal of the European Communities*, C 2, 6 Jan. 1998: 2–5.

Economist, The (1997), 'Disappearing Taxes', *The Economist*, 31 May: 17–19.

EHLERMANN, CLAUS-DIETER (1984), 'How Flexible Is Community Law? An Unusual Approach to the Concept of Two Speeds', *Michigan Law Review*, 82: 1274–93.

——(1995), Comment on Manfred E. Streit and Werner Mussler, 'The Economic Constitution of the European Community: From "Rome" to "Maastricht"', *European Law Journal*, 1: 84–5.

EHMKE, HORST (1961), *Wirtschaft und Verfassung: Die Verfassungsrechtsprechung des Supreme Court zur Wirtschaftsregulierung*. Karlsruhe: C. F. Müller.

EICHENER, VOLKER (1992), 'Social Dumping or Innovative Regulation? Processes and Outcomes of European Decision-Making in the Sector of Health and Safety at Work Harmonization'. EUI Working Paper SPS 92/28. Florence: European University Institute.

——(1993), 'Entscheidungsprozesse bei der Harmonisierung der Technik in der Europäischen Gemeinschaft: Soziales Dumping oder innovativer Arbeitsschutz?', in Werner Süß and Gerhard Becher (eds.), *Politik und Technikentwicklung in Europa: Analysen ökonomisch-technischer und politischer Vermittlung im Prozeß der europäischen Integration*. Berlin: Duncker & Humblot, 207–35.

——(1997), 'Effective European Problem-Solving: Lessons from the Regulation of Occupational Safety and of Environmental Protection', *Journal of European Public Policy*, 4: 591–608.

EICHENGREEN, BARRY (1996), 'Institutions and Economic Growth after World War II', in Nicholas Crafts and Gianni Toniolo (eds.), *Economic Growth since 1945*. Cambridge: Cambridge University Press, 38–72.

EL-AGRAA, ALI M. (ed.) (1990), *The Economics of the European Community*. 3rd edn. New York: St Martin's Press.

EMERSON, MICHAEL, AUJEAN, MICHEL, CATINAT, MICHEL, GOYBET, PHILIPPE, and JACQUEMIN, ALEXIS (1988), *The Economics of 1992: The E.C. Commission's Assessment of the Economic Effects of Completing the Internal Market*. Oxford: Oxford University Press.

ENGEL, CHRISTIAN, and BORRMANN, CHRISTINE (1991), *Vom Konsens zur Mehrheitsentscheidung: EG-Entscheidungsverfahren und national Interessenpolitik nach der Einheitlichen Europäischen Akte*. Bonn: Europa Union Verlag.

ESPING-ANDERSEN, GØSTA (1990), *The Three Worlds of Welfare Capitalism*. Cambridge: Polity Press.

——(ed.) (1996), *Welfare States in Transition*. London: Sage.

——(1997), 'Welfare States at the End of the Century: The Impact of Labour Market, Family, and Demographic Change'. Paper presented at the OECD High Level Conference 'Beyond 2000: The New Social Policy Agenda'. Paris, 12–13 Nov.

European Commission (1990), *Community Charter of the Fundamental Social Rights of Workers*. Luxembourg: Office for Official Publications of the European Communities.

FITOUSSI, JEAN-PAUL (1994), 'Wage Distribution and Unemployment: The French Experience'. *American Economic Review*, 84 (2): 59–64.

FLORA, PETER (ed.) (1986), *Growth to Limits: The Western European Welfare States since World War II*. Berlin: de Gruyter.

FREEMAN, RICHARD B. (1995*a*), 'The Limits of Wage Flexibility in Curing Unemployment', *Oxford Review of Economic Policy*, 11: 63–72.

——(1995*b*), 'The Large Welfare State as a System', *American Economic Review*, 85 (2): 16–21.

FRIEDBACHER, TODD J. (1996), 'Motive Unmasked: The European Court of Justice, the Free Movement of Goods, and the Search for Legitimacy', *European Law Journal*, 2: 226–50.

GARRETT, GEOFFREY (1992), 'International Cooperation and Institutional Choice: The European Community's Internal Market', *International Organization*, 46: 533–60.

——(1995*a*), 'Capital Mobility, Trade, and the Domestic Politics of Economic Policy', *International Organization*, 49: 657–87.

——(1995*b*), 'The Politics of Legal Integration in the European Union', *International Organization*, 49: 171–81.

——(1996), 'Capital Mobility, Trade, and the Domestic Politics of Economic Policy', in Robert O. Keohane and Helen V. Milner (eds.), *Internationalization and Domestic Politics*. Cambridge: Cambridge University Press, 79–107.

——(1998), *Partisan Politics in the Global Economy*. Cambridge: Cambridge University Press.

GENSCHEL, PHILIPP (1998), 'Markt und Staat in Europa'. MPIfG Working Paper 98/1. Cologne: Max Planck Institute for the Study of Societies. Available at: http://www.mpi-fg-koeln.mpg.de.

——and PLÜMPER, THOMAS (1997), 'Regulatory Competition and International Cooperation', *Journal of European Public Policy*, 4: 626–42.

GERBER, DAVID J. (1988), 'Constitutionalizing the Economy: German Neo-liberalism, Competition Law and the "New" Europe', *American Journal of Comparative Law*, 42: 25–84.

——(1994), 'The Transformation of European Community Competition Law?', *Harvard International Law Journal*, 35: 97–147.

GIERING, CLAUS (1997), 'Flexibilisierungskonzepte für Europa'. Arbeitspapier der Forschungsgruppe Europa. Munich: Centrum für angewandte Politikforschung, Universität München.

GIERSCH, HERBERT (1997), 'Das Jahrhundert der Globalisierung: Der Standortwettbewerb bringt nicht das Ende der Wirtschaftspolitik: Aber am Ende ist eine Politik, die den Marktkräften entgegenwirken will', *Frankfurter Allgemeine Zeitung*, 11 Jan.: 13.

GILPIN, ROBERT (1987), *The Political Economy of International Relations*. Princeton: Princeton University Press.

GOLUB, JONATHAN (1996*a*), 'The Politics of Judicial Discretion:

Rethinking the Interaction between National Courts and the European Court of Justice', *West European Politics*, 19: 360–85.

—— (1996*b*), 'Sovereignty and Subsidiarity in EU Environmental Policy', *Political Studies*, 44: 686–703.

—— (1996*c*), 'State Power and Institutional Influence in European Integration: Lessons from the Packaging Waste Directive', *Journal of Common Market Studies*, 34: 313–39.

—— (1996*d*), 'Why Did They Sign? Explaining EC Environmental Bargaining'. EUI Working Paper RSC 96/52. Florence: European University Institute.

—— (1997*a*), 'In the Shadow of the Vote? Decisionmaking Efficiency in the European Community 1974–1995'. MPIfG Discussion Paper 97/3. Cologne: Max Planck Institute for the Study of Societies. Available at: http://www.mpi-fg-koeln.mpg.de.

—— (ed.) (1997*b*), *Global Competition and EU Environmental Policy*. London: Routledge.

GORDON, ROGER H., and BOVENBERG, LANS A. (1996), 'Why is Capital So Immobile Internationally? Possible Explanations and Implications for Capital Income Taxation', *American Economic Review*, 86: 1057–75.

GRABITZ, EBERHARD (ed.) (1984), *Abgestufte Integration: Eine Alternative zum herkömmlichen Integrationskonzept*. Kehl: Engel.

GRANDE, EDGAR (1996), 'Demokratische Legitimation und europäische Integration', *Leviathan*, 24: 339–60.

GROEBEN, HANS VON DER (1992), 'Probleme einer europäischen Wirtschaftsordnung', in Jürgen F. Baur, Peter-Christian Müller-Graff, and Manfred Zuleeg (eds.), *Europarecht, Energierecht, Wirtschaftsrecht: Festschrift für Bodo Börner*. Cologne: Carl Heymanns, 99–123.

—— (1996), 'Ernst-Joachim Mestmäckers Beitrag zur Gestaltung einer europäischen Wettbewerbspolitik', in Ulrich Immenga, Werner Mösche, and Dieter Reuter (eds.), *Festschrift für Ernst-Joachim Mestmäcker zum 70. Geburtstag*. Baden-Baden: Nomos, 29–40.

GUÉHENNO, JEAN-MARIE (1993), *La Fin de la démocratie*. Paris: Flammarion.

HAAS, ERNST B. (1980), 'Why Collaborate? Issue Linkage and International Regimes', *World Politics*, 32: 357–405.

HAAS, PETER M. (1992), 'Introduction: Epistemic Communities and International Policy Coordination', *International Organization*, 46: 1–35.

HABERMAS, JÜRGEN (1973), *Legitimationsprobleme im Spätkapitalismus*. Frankfurt am Main: Suhrkamp.

——(1976), *Legitimation Crisis*. London: Heinemann.

——(1989), 'Towards a Communication Concept of Rational Collective Will-Formation: A Thought Experiment', *Ratio juris*, 2: 144–54.

——(1996), *Die Einbeziehung des Anderen: Studien zur politischen Theorie*. Frankfurt am Main: Suhrkamp.

HANCHER, LEIGH (1995), 'Case C-393/92, Gemeente Almelo and Others v. Energiebedijf Ijsselmij NV', *Common Market Law Review*, 32: 305–25.

HAND, LEARNED (1960), *The Spirit of Liberty*. Cambridge, Mass.: Harvard University Press.

HANESCH, WALTER (1995), 'Sozialpolitik und arbeitsmarktbedingte Armut: Strukturmängel und Reformbedarf in der sozialen Sicherung bei Arbeitslosigkeit', *Aus Politik und Zeitgeschichte*, B 31–2/95: 14–23.

HARDIN, GARRETT (1968), 'The Tragedy of the Commons', *Science*, 162: 1243–68.

HÄRTEL, HANS-HAGEN (1997), 'Fehlsteuerung durch Lohnnebenkosten', *Wirtschaftsdienst*, 77: 370–2.

HAVEMAN, ROBERT (1997), 'Employment and Social Protection: Are They Compatible?' Paper presented at the OECD High Level Conference 'Beyond 2000: The New Social Policy Agenda'. Paris, 12–13 Nov.

HAYEK, FRIEDRICH A. (1944), *The Road to Serfdom*. Chicago: University of Chicago Press.

——(1945), 'The Use of Knowledge in Society', *American Economic Review*, 35: 519–30.

HAYES-RENSHAW, FIONA, and WALLACE, HELEN (1997), *The Council of Ministers*. London: Macmillan.

HENNIS, WILHELM, et al. (1977), *Regierbarkeit: Studien zu ihrer Problematisierung*, vol. i. Stuttgart: Klett.

——et al. (1979), *Regierbarkeit: Studien zu ihrer Problematisierung*, vol. ii. Stuttgart: Klett.

HÉRITIER, ADRIENNE (1993), 'Policy-Netzwerkanalyse als Untersuchungsinstrument im europäischen Kontext: Folgerungen aus einer empirischen Studie regulativer Politik', in Adrienne Héritier (ed.), *Policy-Analyse: Kritik und Neuorientierung*. Politische Vierteljahresschrift Sonderheft 24. Opladen: Westdeutscher Verlag, 432–47.

——(1997), 'Market-Making Policy in Europe: Its Impact on Member-State Policies: The Case of Road Haulage in Britain, the Netherlands, Germany and Italy', *Journal of European Public Policy*, 4: 539–55.

——KNILL, CHRISTOPH, and MINGERS, SUSANNE (1996), *Ringing the Changes in Europe: Regulatory Competition and Redefinition of the State: Britain, France, Germany*. Berlin: de Gruyter.

HIRST, PAUL, and THOMPSON, GRAHAME (1995), 'Globalization and the Future of the Nation State', *Economy and Society*, 24: 408–42.

HOEKMAN, BERNARD M., and KOSTECKI, MICHAEL (1995), *The Political Economy of the World Trading System: From GATT to WTO*. Oxford: Oxford University Press.

HOLLINGSWORTH, J. ROGERS, and BOYER, ROBERT (eds.) (1997), *Contemporary Capitalism: The Embeddedness of Institutions*. Cambridge: Cambridge University Press.

HOLMES, OLIVER WENDELL, Jr. (1881), *The Common Law*. Boston: Little, Brown.

HOSLI, MADELEINE (1996), 'Coalitions and Power. Effects of Qualified Majority Voting on the Council of the European Union', *Journal of Common Market Studies*, 34: 255–74.

HÜTHER, MICHAEL (1990), *Integrierte Steuer-Transfer-Systeme für die Bundesrepublik Deutschland: Normative Konzeption und empirische Analyse*. Berlin: Duncker & Humblot.

IRELAND, PATRICK R. (1995), 'Migration, Free Movement, and Immigrant Immigration in the EU: A Bifurcated Policy Response', in Stephan Leibfried and Paul Pierson (eds.), *European Social Policy: Between Fragmentation and Integration*. Washington: Brookings, 231–66.

JACHTENFUCHS, MARKUS, and KOHLER-KOCH, BEATE (1996), 'Einleitung: Regieren im dynamischen Mehrebenensystem', in Markus Jachtenfuchs and Beate Kohler-Koch (eds.), *Europäische Integration*. Opladen: Leske & Budrich, 15–44.

JACQUEMIN, ALEXIS, and WRIGHT, DAVID (eds.) (1993), *The European Challenges Post-1992*. Aldershot: Elgar.

JOERGES, CHRISTIAN (1991), 'Markt ohne Staat? Die Wirtschaftsverfassung der Gemeinschaft und die regulative Politik', in Rudolf Wildenmann (ed.), *Staatswerdung Europas? Optionen für eine Europäische Union*. Baden-Baden: Nomos, 225–68.

——(1994*a*), 'European Economic Law, the Nation-State and the Maastricht Treaty', in Renaud Dehousse (ed.), *Europe after Maastricht: An Ever Closer Union?* Munich: Beck, 29–62.

——(1994*b*), 'Rationalisierungsprozesse im Vertragsrecht und im Recht der Produktsicherheit: Beobachtungen zu den Folgen der europäischen Integration für das Privatrecht'. EUI Working Papers LAW 94/5. Florence: European University Institute.

——(1996), 'Das Recht im Prozeß der europäischen Integration', in Markus Jachtenfuchs and Beate Kohler-Koch (eds.), *Europäische Integration*. Opladen: Leske & Budrich, 73–108.

——(1997), 'The Impact of European Integration on Private Law: Reductionist Perceptions, True Conflicts and a New Constitutionalist Perspective', *European Law Journal*, 3: 378–406.

——and NEYER, JÜRGEN (1997), 'Transforming Strategic Interaction into Deliberative Problem-Solving: European Comitology in the Foodstuffs Sector', *Journal of European Public Policy*, 4: 609–25.

KAPSTEIN, ETHAN B. (1994), *Governing the Global Economy: International Finance and the State*. Cambridge, Mass.: Harvard University Press.

KAPTEYN, PAUL (1991), '"Civilization under Negotiation": National Civilizations and European Integration: The Treaty of Schengen', *Archives européennes de sociologie*, 32: 363–80.

——(1996), *The Stateless Market: The European Dilemma of Integration and Civilization*. London: Routledge.

KASSIM, HUSSEIN (1994), 'Policy Networks and European Union Policy Making: A Skeptical View', *West European Politics*, 17: 15–27.

KEOHANE, ROBERT O. (1984), *After Hegemony: Cooperation and Discord in the World Political Economy*. Princeton: Princeton University Press.

——and OSTROM, ELINOR (1994), 'Local Commons and Global Interdependence: Heterogeneity and Cooperation in Two Domains. Introduction', *Journal of Theoretical Politics*, 6: 403–28.

KINDLEBERGER, CHARLES P. (1973), *The World in Depression 1929–1939*. London: Allen Lane.

——(1978), *Manias, Panics, and Crashes: A History of Financial Crises*. New York: Basic Books.

——(1995), *The World Economy and National Finance in Historical Perspective*. Ann Arbor: University of Michigan Press.

KISER, LARRY L., and OSTROM, ELINOR (1982), 'The Three Worlds of Action: A Metatheoretical Synthesis of Institutional Approaches', in Elinor Ostrom (ed.), *Strategies of Political Inquiry*. Beverly Hills, Calif.: Sage, 179–222.

KLEINSTEUBER, HANS, and ROSSMANN, TORSTEN (1994), *Europa als Kommunikationsraum: Akteure, Strukturen und Konfliktpotentiale*. Opladen: Leske & Budrich.

KNOKE, DAVID (1990), 'Networks of Political Action: Towards Theory Construction', *Social Forces*, 68: 1041–63.

——PAPPI, FRANZ URBAN, BROADBENT, JEFFREY, and TSUJINAKA, YUTAKA (1996), *Comparing Policy Networks: Labour Politics in the U.S., Germany, and Japan*. Cambridge: Cambridge University Press.

KOMESAR, NEIL (1994), *Imperfect Alternatives: Choosing Institutions in Law, Economics and Public Policy*. Chicago: University of Chicago Press.

KORPI, WALTER (1983), *The Democratic Class Struggle*. London: Routledge & Kegan Paul.

KOSONEN, PEKKA (1994), 'The Impact of Economic Integration on

National Welfare States in Europe'. MS. Helsinki: Department of Sociology of Law, University of Helsinki.

LADEUR, KARL-HEINZ (1992), 'Die Autonomie der Bundesbank: Ein Beispiel für die institutionelle Verarbeitung von Ungewißheits-bedingungen', *Staatswissenschaften und Staatspraxis*, 4: 486–508.

——(1997), 'Towards a Legal Theory of Supranationality: The Viability of the Network Concept', *European Law Journal*, 3: 33–54.

LAHR, ROLF (1983), 'Die Legende vom "Luxemburger Kompromiß"', *Europa-Archiv*, 38: 223–32.

LANGEHEINE, BERND, and WEINSTOCK, ULRICH (1984), 'Abgestufte Integration: Weder Königsweg noch Irrweg: Zur Auseinandersetzung über die Weiterentwicklung der Europäischen Gemeinschaft', *Europa-Archiv*, 39: 261–70.

LAUMANN, EDWARD O., and KNOKE, DAVID (1989), 'Policy Networks of the Organizational State: Collective Action in the National Energy and Health Domains', in Robert Perrucci and Harry R. Potter (eds.), *Networks of Power: Organizational Actors at the National, Corporate, and Community Levels*. New York: Aldine de Gruyter, 17–55.

LEIBFRIED, STEPHAN, and RIEGER, ELMAR (1997), 'Limits to Globalization: Welfare State Reasons for Economic Openness or Closure'. MS. Stanford, Calif.: European Forum, Stanford University.

LEWIS, JEFFREY (1997), 'The Institutional Problem-Solving Capacities of the Council: The Committee of Permanent Representatives and the Methods of Community'. MPIfG Discussion Paper 98/1. Cologne: Max Planck Institute for the Study of Societies. Available at: http://www.mpi-fg-koeln.mpg.de.

LINDBLOM, CHARLES E. (1965), *The Intelligence of Democracy: Decision Making through Mutual Adjustment*. New York: Free Press.

LÜTZ, SUSANNE (1996), 'The Revival of the Nation State? Stock Exchange Regulation in an Era of Internationalized Financial Markets'. MPIfG Discussion Paper 96/9. Cologne: Max Planck Institute for the Study of Societies. Available at: http://www.mpi-fg-koeln.mpg.de.

MADURO, MIGUEL POIARES (1997), 'Reforming the Market or the State? Article 30 and the European Constitution: Economic Freedom and Political Rights', *European Law Journal*, 3: 55–82.

MAJONE, GIANDOMENICO (1989), *Evidence, Argument, and Persuasion in the Policy Process*. New Haven: Yale University Press.

——(1993), 'The European Community between Social Policy and Social Regulation', *Journal of Common Market Studies*, 31: 153–70.

——(1996a), *Regulating Europe*. London: Routledge.

——(1996b), 'Regulatory Legitimacy', in Giandomenico Majone, *Regulating Europe*. London: Routledge, 284–301.

MARIN, BERND, and MAYNTZ, RENATE (eds.) (1991), *Policy Networks: Empirical Evidence and Theoretical Considerations*. Frankfurt am Main: Campus.

MARKS, GARY (1993), 'Structural Policy and Multilevel Governance in the EC', in Alan Cafruni and Glenda Rosenthal (eds.), *The State of the European Community: The Maastricht Debates and Beyond*. Boulder, Colo.: Lynne Rienner, 391–410.

——NIELSEN, FRANÇOIS, RAY, LEONARD, and SALK, JANE (1996), 'Competencies, Cracks and Conflicts: Regional Mobilization in the European Union', in Gary Marks, Fritz W. Scharpf, Philippe C. Schmitter, and Wolfgang Streeck, *Governance in the European Union*. London: Sage, 40–63.

MARSHALL, THOMAS H. (1975), *Social Policy*. London: Hutchinson.

MATTLI, WALTER, and SLAUGHTER, ANNE-MARIE (1995), 'Law and Politics in the European Union: A Reply to Garrett', *International Organization*, 49: 183–90.

MAYNTZ, RENATE, and SCHARPF, FRITZ W. (1995a), 'Der Ansatz des akteurzentrierten Institutionalismus', in Renate Mayntz and Fritz W. Scharpf (eds.), *Gesellschaftliche Selbstregelung und politische Steuerung*. Frankfurt am Main: Campus, 39–72.

——(1995b), 'Steuerung und Selbstorganisation in staatsnahen Sektoren', in Renate Mayntz and Fritz W. Scharpf (eds.), *Gesellschaftliche Selbstregelung und politische Steuerung*. Frankfurt am Main: Campus, 9–38.

MAZEY, SONIA, and RICHARDSON, JEREMY (eds.) (1993), *Lobbying in the European Community*. Oxford: Oxford University Press.

MENDRINOU, MARIA (1996), 'Non-compliance and the European Commission's Role in Integration', *Journal of European Public Policy*, 3: 1–22.

MERKEL, WOLFGANG (1993*a*), *Ende der Sozialdemokratie? Machtressourcen und Regierungspolitik im internationalen Vergleich.* Frankfurt am Main: Campus.

——(1993*b*), *Integration and Democracy in the European Community: The Contours of a Dilemma.* Estudio 1993/42. Madrid: Instituto Juan March.

MESTMÄCKER, ERNST-JOACHIM (1987), 'Auf dem Wege zu einer Ordnungspolitik für Europa', in Ernst-Joachim Mestmäcker, Hans Möller, and Hans-Peter Schwarz (eds.), *Eine Ordnungspolitik für Europa: Festschrift für Hans von der Groeben zu seinem 80. Geburtstag.* Baden-Baden: Nomos, 9–49.

——(1992), 'Widersprüchlich, verwirrend und gefährlich: Wettbewerbsregeln oder Industriepolitik: Nicht nur in diesem Punkt verstößt der Vertrag von Maastricht gegen bewährte Grundsätze des Vertrages von Rom', *Frankfurter Allgemeine Zeitung*, 10 Oct.: 15.

——(1994), 'Zur Wirtschaftsverfassung in der Europäischen Union', in Rolf H. Hasse, Josef Molsberger, and Christian Watrin (eds.), *Ordnung in Freiheit: Festgabe für Hans Willgerodt zum 70. Geburtstag.* Stuttgart: Fischer, 263–92.

MILLER, DAVID (1993), 'Deliberative Democracy and Social Choice', in David Held (ed.), *Prospects for Democracy: North, South, East, West.* Cambridge: Polity Press, 74–92.

MITCHELL, RONALD B. (1994), 'Heterogeneities at Two Levels: States, Non-state Actors and Intentional Oil Pollution', *Journal of Theoretical Politics*, 6: 625–53.

MITSCHKE, JOACHIM (1985), *Steuer- und Transferordnung aus einem Guß: Entwurf einer Neugestaltung der direkten Steuern und Sozialtransfers in der Bundesrepublik Deutschland.* Baden-Baden: Nomos.

——(1995), 'Steuer- und Sozialpolitik für mehr reguläre Beschäftigung', *Wirtschaftsdienst*, 75: 75–84.

MORAVCSIK, ANDREW (1993), 'Preferences and Power in the

European Community: A Liberal Intergovernmentalist Approach', *Journal of Common Market Studies*, 31: 473–524.

——(1994), 'Why the European Community Strengthens the State: Domestic Politics and International Cooperation'. Working Paper 52. Cambridge, Mass.: Center for European Studies, Harvard University.

MOUSSIS, NICHOLAS (1994), *Handbook of the European Union: Institutions and Policies*. Rixensart: EDIT-EUR.

MÜLLER-ARMACK, ALFRED (1966), 'Soziale Marktwirtschaft', in Alfred Müller-Armack, *Wirtschaftsordnung und Wirtschaftspolitik: Studien und Konzepte zur sozialen Marktwirtschaft und zur europäischen Integration*. Freiburg im Breisgau: Rombach, 243–9.

NEUBÄUMER, RENATE (1997), 'Hat Westdeutschland ein Standortproblem?', *Wirtschaftsdienst*, 77: 408–15.

NICOLL, WILLIAM (1984), 'Paths to European Unity', *Journal of Common Market Studies*, 23: 199–206.

NORRIE, KENNETH, SIMEON, RICHARD, and KRASNICK, MARK (1986), *Federalism and the Economic Union in Canada*. Toronto: University of Toronto Press.

OECD (1994), *The OECD Jobs Study: Facts, Analysis, Strategies*. Paris: OECD.

——(1995), *Income Distribution in OECD Countries*. Social Policy Studies No. 18. Paris: OECD.

——(1996a), *Employment Outlook, July 1996*. Paris: OECD.

——(1996b), 'Social Expenditure Statistics of OECD Member Countries: Provisional Version'. Labour Market and Social Policy Occasional Papers No. 17. Paris: OECD.

——(1996c), *Historical Statistics 1960–1994*. Paris: OECD.

——(1997a), *National Accounts 1983–1995: Detailed Tables Volume II*. Paris: OECD.

——(1997b), *Family, Market and Community: Equity and Efficiency in Social Policy*. Social Policy Studies 21. Paris: OECD.

——(1997c), *Labour Force Statistics 1976–1996*. Paris: OECD.

——(1997d), 'Economic Performance and the Structure of Collective Bargaining', *Employment Outlook, July 1997*. Paris: OECD, 63–92.

OFFE, CLAUS (1972), *Strukturprobleme des kapitalistischen Staates.* Frankfurt am Main: Suhrkamp.

——(1984), *Contradictions of the Welfare State.* London: Hutchinson.

——(1998), 'Demokratie und Wohlfahrtsstaat: Eine europäische Regimeform unter dem Streß der europäischen Itegration', in Wolfgang Streeck (ed.), *Internationale Wirtschaft und nationale Demokratie: Herausforderungen für die Demokratietheorie.* Frankfurt am Main: Campus, forthcoming.

OLSON, MANCUR (1965), *The Logic of Collective Action: Public Goods and the Theory of Groups.* Cambridge, Mass.: Harvard University Press.

——(1982), *The Rise and Decline of Nations: Economic Growth, Stagflation, and Social Rigidities.* New Haven: Yale University Press.

OSTNER, ILONA, and LEWIS, JANE (1995), 'Gender and the Evolution of European Social Policies', in Stephan Leibfried and Paul Pierson (eds.), *European Social Policy: Between Fragmentation and Integration.* Washington: Brookings, 159–93.

OYE, KENNETH A., and MAXWELL, JAMES H. (1994), 'Self-Interest and Environmental Management', *Journal of Theoretical Politics,* 6: 593–624.

PAPPI, FRANZ URBAN, and SCHNORPFEIL, WILLI (1996), 'Das Ausschußwesen der Europäischen Kommission: Grundstrukturen und Kommunikationsmöglichkeiten für Verbände, in Thomas König, Elmar Rieger, and Hermann Schmitt (eds.), *Das europäische Mehrebenensystem.* Frankfurt am Main: Campus, 135–59.

PEDLER, ROBIN H., and SCHAEFER, GUENTHER F. (eds.) (1996), *Shaping European Law and Policy: The Role of Committees and Comitology in the Political Process.* Maastricht: European Institute of Public Administration.

PETERSON, JOHN (1995), 'Policy Networks and European Union Policy-Making: A Reply to Kassim', *West European Politics,* 18: 389–407.

PHELPS, EDMUND S. (1997), 'Wage Subsidy Programs: Alternative Designs', in Dennis J. Snower and Guillermo de la Dehesa (eds.),

Unemployment Policy: Government Options for the Labour Market. Cambridge: Cambridge University Press, 206–44.

PIERSON, PAUL (1994), *Dismantling the Welfare State? Reagan, Thatcher, and the Politics of Retrenchment.* Cambridge: Cambridge University Press.

——(1996), 'The New Politics of the Welfare State', *World Politics*, 48: 147–79.

PITSCHAS, RAINER (1994), 'Europäische Integration als Netzwerk-koordination Komplexer Staatsaufgaben', *Staatswissenschaften und Staatspraxis*, 5: 503–40.

POLANYI, KARL (1957), *The Great Transformation: The Political and Economic Origins of our Time.* Boston: Beacon Press.

POLLACK, MARK A. (1997*a*), 'Delegation, Agency, and Agenda Setting in the European Community', *International Organization*, 51: 99–134.

——(1997*b*), 'Representing Diffuse Interests in EC Policymaking', *Journal of European Public Policy*, 4: 572–90.

PUTNAM, ROBERT D. (1996), 'Symptome der Krise: Die USA, Europa und Japan im Vergleich', in Werner Weidenfeld (ed.), *Demokratie am Wendepunkt: Die demokratische Frage als Projekt des 21. Jahrhunderts.* Berlin: Siedler, 52–80.

RASCH, STEFFEN (1996), 'Perspektiven für eine einheitliche Zinsbesteuerung in der EU', in Thomas König, Elmar Rieger, and Hermann Schmitt (eds.), *Das europäische Mehrebenensystem.* Frankfurt am Main: Campus, 315–31.

REHBINDER, ECKARD, and STEWART, RICHARD (1984), *Environmental Protection Policy: Integration through Law: Europe and the American Federal Experience.* Vol. ii. Berlin: de Gruyter.

REICH, NORBERT (1994), 'The "November Revolution" of the European Court of Justice: Keck, Meng and Audi Revistited', *Common Market Law Review*, 31: 459–92.

RHODES, MARTIN (1996), 'A New Social Contract? Globalization and West European Welfare States'. EUI Working Paper RSC 96/43. Florence: European University Institute.

RIKER, WILLIAM H. (1982), *Liberalism against Populism: A Confrontation between the Theory of Democracy and the Theory of Social Choice.* San Francisco: W. H. Freeman.

[221]

RÖPKE, WILHELM (1942), *International Economic Disintegration*. London: William Hodge.

ROSS, GEORGE (1995), *Jacques Delors and European Integration*. Cambridge: Polity Press.

ROTHERMUND, DIETMAR (1993), *Die Welt in der Wirtschaftskrise 1929–1939*. Münster: Lit.

RUGGIE, JOHN GERARD (1982), 'International Regimes, Transactions, and Change: Embedded Liberalism in the Postwar Economic Order', *International Organization*, 36: 379–415.

——(1994), 'Trade, Protectionism and the Future of Welfare Capitalism', *Journal of International Affairs*, 48: 1–11.

RUNCIMAN, WALTER G., and SEN, AMARTYA K. (1965), 'Games, Justice and the General Will', *Mind*, 74: 554–62.

SCHARPF, FRITZ W. (1966), 'Judicial Review and the Political Question: A Functional Analysis', *Yale Law Journal*, 75: 517–97.

——(1970a), *Demokratietheorie zwischen Utopie und Anpassung*. Konstanz: Universitätsverlag.

——(1970b), *Die politischen Kosten des Rechtsstaats: Eine vergleichende Studie der deutschen und amerikanischen Verwaltungskontrollen*. Tübingen: Mohr.

——(1988), 'The Joint Decision Trap: Lessons from German Federalism and European Integration', *Public Administration*, 66: 239–78.

——(1991), *Crisis and Choice in European Social Democracy*. Ithaca, NY: Cornell University Press.

——(1992), 'Koordination durch Verhandlungssysteme: Analytische Konzepte und institutionelle Lösungen', in Arthur Benz, Fritz W. Scharpf, and Reinhard Zintl, *Horizontale Politikverflechtung: Zur Theorie von Verhandlungssystemen*. Frankfurt am Main: Campus, 51–96.

——(1993), 'Von der Finanzierung der Arbeitslosigkeit zur Subventionierung niedriger Erwerbseinkommen', *Gewerkschaftliche Monatshefte*, 44: 433–43.

——(1994), 'Community and Autonomy: Multi-level Policy Making in the European Union', *Journal of European Public Policy*, 1: 219–42.

——(1995), 'Federal Arrangements and Multi-party Systems', *Australian Journal of Political Science*, 30: 27–39.

——(1996), 'Negative and Positive Integration in the Political Economy of European Welfare States', in Gary Marks, Fritz W. Scharpf, Philippe C. Schmitter, and Wolfgang Streeck, *Governance in the European Union*. London: Sage, 15–39.

——(1997*a*), *Games Real Actors Play: Actor-Centered Institutionalism in Policy Research*. Boulder, Colo.: Westview.

——(1997*b*), 'Economic Integration, Democracy and the Welfare State', *Journal of European Public Policy*, 4: 18–36.

——(1997*c*), 'Introduction: The Problem Solving Capacity of Multi-level Governance', *Journal of European Public Policy*, 4: 520–38.

SCHMALZ-BRUNS, RAINER (1995), *Reflexive Demokratie: Die demokratische Transformation moderner Politik*. Baden-Baden: Nomos.

SCHMID, GÜNTHER (1996), 'The Dutch Emploment Miracle? A Comparison of Employment Systems in the Netherlands and Germany'. Discussion Paper FS 96-206. Berlin: Wissenschaftszentrum für Sozialforschung.

SCHMID, JOSEF (1996), *Wohlfahrtsstaaten im Vergleich: Soziale Sicherungssysteme in Europa: Organisation, Finanzierung, Leistungen und Probleme*. Opladen: Leske & Budrich.

SCHMIDT, SUSANNE K. (1996), 'Sterile Debates and Dubious Generalizations: European Integration Theory Tested by Telecommunications and Electricity', *Journal of Public Policy*, 16: 233–71.

——(1997*a*), 'Behind the Council Agenda: The Commission's Impact on Decisions'. MPIfG Discussion Paper 97/4. Cologne: Max Planck Institute for the Study of Societies. Available at: http://www.mpi-fg-koeln.mpg.de.

——(1997*b*), 'Die wettbewerbsrechtliche Handlungsfähigkeit der Europäischen Kommission in staatsnahen Sektoren'. Dissertation. Published as: 'Liberalisierung in Europa. Die Rolle der Europäischen Kommission'. Frankfurt am Main, 1998.

——(1998), 'Commission Activism: Subsuming Telecommunications and Electricity under European Competition Law', *Journal of European Public Policy*, 5: 169–84.

SCHMIDT, VIVIEN (1997), 'European Integration and Democracy: The Differences among Member States', *Journal of European Public Policy*, 4: 128–45.

SCHNEIDER, VOLKER (1995), 'Institutionelle Evolution als politischer Prozeß: Die Entwicklung der Telekommunikation im internationalen und historischen Vergleich'. MS. Cologne: Max Planck Institute for the Study of Societies.

SCHUBERT, GLENDON A. (1996), *Constitutional Politics: The Political Behavior of Supreme Court Justices and the Constitutional Policies that They Make*. New York: Holt, Rinehart & Winston.

SHEPSLE, KENNETH A., and WEINGAST, BARRY R. (1987), 'The Institutional Foundations of Committee Power', *American Political Science Review*, 81: 85–104.

SINN, HANS-WERNER (1994), 'Wieviel Brüssel braucht Europa? Subsidiarität, Zentralisierung und Fiskalwettbewerb im Lichte der ökonomischen Theorie', *Staatswissenschaften und Staatspraxis*, 5: 155–86.

—— (1996), 'The Subsidiarily Principle and Market Failure in Systems Competition'. CES Working Paper 103. Munich: Centre for Economic Studies.

SINN, STEFAN (1993), 'The Taming of Leviathan: Competition among Governments', *Constitutional Political Economy*, 3: 177–221.

SLOOT, THOMAS, and VERSCHUREN, PIET (1990), 'Decision-Making Speed in the European Community', *Journal of Common Market Studies*, 29: 75–85.

SMITH, ALASDAIR, and VENABLES, ANTHONY (1988), 'The Costs of Non-Europe: An Assessment Based on a Formal Model of Imperfect Competition and the Economies of Scale'. Economic Papers 70. Brussels: Commission of the European Communities.

SÖDERSTEN, BO, and REED, GEOFFREY (1994), *International Economics*. 3rd edn. New York: St Martin's Press.

SOLOW, ROBERT M. (1997), 'Is There a Core of Usable Macroeconomics We Should All Believe in?', *American Economic Review*, 87 (2): 230–2.

SOSKICE, DAVID (1990), 'Wage Determination: The Changing Role of Institutions in Advanced Industrial Countries', *Oxford Review of Economic Policy*, 6: 36–61.

STEINMO, SVEN (1994), 'The End of Redistribution? International Pressures and Domestic Policy Choices', *Challenge*, 37 (6): 9–17.

STEWART, RICHARD B. (1993), 'Environmental Regulation and International Competitiveness', *Yale Law Journal*, 102: 2039–106.

STREECK, WOLFGANG (1992), *Social Institutions and Economic Performance: Studies of Industrial Relations in Advanced Capitalist Economies*. London: Sage.

——(1995*a*), 'From Market-Making to State-Building? Reflections on the Political Economy of European Social Policy', in Stephan Leibfried and Paul Pierson (eds.), *European Social Policy: Between Fragmentation and Integration*. Washington: Brookings, 389–431.

——(1995*b*), 'Neo-voluntarism: A New European Social Policy Regime?', *European Law Journal*, 1: 31–59.

——(1996), 'Gewerkschaften zwischen Nationalstaat und Europäischer Union'. MPIfG Working Paper 96/1. Cologne: Max Planck Institute for the Study of Societies. Available at: http://www.mpi-fg-koeln.mpg.de.

——(1997*a*), 'German Capitalism: Does It Exist? Can It Survive?', *New Political Economy*, 2: 237–56.

——(1997*b*), 'Industrial Citizenship under Regime Competition: The Case of European Works Councils', *Journal of European Public Policy*, 4: 643–64.

——(1998), 'The Germany-Japan Project: Where We Are'. MS. Cologne: Max Planck Institute for the Study of Societies.

——and SCHMITTER, PHILIPPE C. (1991), 'From National Corporatism to Transnational Pluralism: Organized Interests in the Single European Market', *Politics and Society*, 19: 133–64.

STREIT, MANFRED E. (1993), 'Cognition, Competition, and Catallaxy: In Memory of Friedrich August von Hayek', *Constitutional Political Economy*, 4: 223–62.

——(1996*a*), 'Competition among Systems, Harmonisation and European Integration'. Diskussionsbeitrag 01-96. Jena: Max Planck Institute for Research into Economic Systems.

STREIT, MANFRED E. (1996*b*), 'Systemwettbewerb im europäischen Integrationsprozeß', in Ulrich Immenga, Wernhard Möschel, and Dieter Reuter (eds.), *Festschrift für Ernst-Joachim Mestmäcker zum 70. Geburtstag*. Baden-Baden: Nomos, 521–35.

——and MUSSLER, WERNER (1995), 'The Economic Constitution of the European Community: From "Rome" to "Maastricht"', *European Law Journal*, 1: 5–30.

SWANK, DUANE (1997), 'Funding the Welfare State: Globalization and the Taxation of Business in Advanced Market Economies'. MS. Milwaukee: Marquette University.

TALMON, JACOB L. (1955), *The Origins of Totalitarian Democracy*. London: Secker & Warburg.

TAYLOR, JOHN B. (1997), 'A Core of Practical Macroeconomics', *American Economic Review*, 87 (2): 233–5.

TEASDALE, ANTHONY L. (1993), 'The Life and Death of the Luxembourg Compromise', *Journal of Common Market Studies*, 31: 567–79.

TINBERGEN, JAN (1965), *International Economic Integration*. 2nd edn. Amsterdam: Elsevier.

TINDEMANS, LEO (1975), *Report on the European Union. Bulletin of the European Communities*. Supplement 1/76.

TRUMAN, DAVID B. (1951), *The Governmental Process: Political Interests and Public Opinion*. New York: Knopf.

TSEBELIS, GEORGE (1994), 'The Power of the European Parliament as a Conditional Agenda Setter', *American Political Science Review*, 88: 128–42.

——(1995), 'Decision Making in Political Systems: Comparison of Presidentialism, Parliamentarism, Multicameralism, and Multipartyism', *British Journal of Political Science*, 25: 289–325.

TSOUKALIS, LOUKAS (1997), *The New European Economy Revisited*. Oxford: Oxford University Press.

URWIN, DEREK W. (1991), *The Community of Europe: A History of European Integration since 1945*. 2nd edn. London: Longman.

VERLOREN VAN THEMAAT, PIETER (1987), 'Die Aufgabenverteilung zwischen dem Gesetzgeber und dem Europäischen Gerichtshof bei der Gestaltung der Wirtschaftsverfassung der Europäischen Gemeinschaften', in Ernst-Joachim Mestmäcker, Hans Möller, and Hans-Peter Schwarz (eds.), *Eine Ordnungspolitik für Europa: Festschrift für Hans von der Groeben zu seinem 80. Geburtstag.* Baden-Baden: Nomos, 425–43.

VILLENEUVE, ROBERT (1997), 'The Role of Public Services in Building European Citizenship', *Transfer*, 3: 98–118.

VISSER, JELLE, and EBBINGHAUS, BERHARD (1992), 'Making the Most of Diversity? European Integration and Transnational Organization of Labor', in Justin Greenwood, Jürgen Grote, and Karsten Ronit (eds.), *Organized Interests and the European Community.* London: Sage, 206–38.

——and HEMERIJCK, ANTON (1997), *'A Dutch Miracle': Job Growth, Welfare Reform and Corporatism in the Netherlands.* Amsterdam: Amsterdam University Press.

VOGEL, DAVID (1995), *Trading up: Consumer and Environmental Regulation in a Global Economy.* Cambridge, Mass.: Harvard University Press.

——(1997), 'Trading up and Governing across: Transnational Governance and Environmental Protection', *Journal of European Public Policy*, 4: 556–71.

WALLERSTEIN, MICHAEL (1990), 'Class Conflict as a Dynamic Game', in Roger Friedland and A. F. Robertson (eds.), *Beyond the Marketplace: Rethinking Economy and Society.* New York: Aldine de Gruyter, 189–212.

WARD, HUGH (1993), 'Game Theory and the Politics of the Global Commons', *Journal of Conflict Resolution*, 37: 203–35.

WEBBER, DOUGLAS (1997), 'France, Germany and Agricultural Crisis Politics in the European Union'. Paper prepared for the conference 'The Franco-German Relationship in the European Union: The Hard, the Rotting or the Hollow Core?' Florence, 6–7 Feb.

WEILER, JOSEPH H. H. (1982), 'The Community System: The Dual Character of Supranationalism', *Yearbook of European Law*, 1: 257–306.

——(1992), 'After Maastricht: Community Legitimacy in Post-1992 Europe', in William James Adams (ed.), *Singular Europe: Economy and Polity of the European Community after 1992.* Ann Arbor: University of Michigan Press, 11–41.

[227]

WEILER, JOSEPH H. H. (1994), 'A Quiet Revolution: The European Court of Justice and its Interlocutors', *Comparative Political Studies*, 26: 510–34.

——(1995), 'Does Europe Need a Constitution? Reflection on Demos, Telos and the German Maastricht Decision', *European Law Journal*, 1: 219–58.

——(1997a), 'To Be a European Citizen: Eros and Civilization', *Journal of European Public Policy*, 4: 495–519.

——(1997b), 'The Reformation of European Constitutionalism', *Journal of Common Market Studies*, 35: 97–121.

WEIR, MARGARET (1995), 'Poverty, Social Rights, and the Politics of Place in the United States', in Stephan Leibfried and Paul Pierson (eds.), *European Social Policy: Between Fragmentation and Integration*. Washington: Brookings, 329–54.

WEIZSÄCKER, ERNST-ULRICH VON (1989), 'Internationale Harmonisierung im Umweltschutz durch ökonomische Instrumente: Gründe für eine europäische Umweltsteuer', *Jahrbuch zur Staats- und Verwaltungswissenschaft*, 3: 203–16.

WERLE, RAYMUND (1993), 'Politische Techniksteuerung durch europäische Standardisierung?', in Herbert Kubicek and Peter Seege (eds.), *Perspektive Techniksteuerung: Interdisziplinäre Sichtweisen eines Schlüsselproblems entwickelter Industriegesellschaften*. Berlin: Edition Sigma, 129–42.

——(1997), 'Technische Standardisierung im deregulierenden Europa', in Karl-Ernst Schenk, Dieter Schmidtchen, and Manfred E. Streit (eds.), *Jahrbuch für neue politische Ökonomie*, 16: *Neue politische Ökonomie der Integration und Öffnung von Infrastrukturnetzen*. Tübingen: Mohr, 54–80.

WILENSKY, HAROLD L. (1975), *The Welfare State and Equality: Structural and Ideological Roots of Public Expenditures*. Berkeley and Los Angeles: University of California Press.

WILEY, MARY GLENN, and ZALD, MAYER N. (1968), 'The Growth and Transformation of Educational Accrediting Agencies: An Exploratory Study in Social Control of Institutions', *Sociology of Education*, 41: 36–56.

WILLKE, HELMUT (1983), *Entzauberung des Staates: Überlegungen zu einer sozietalen Steuerungstheorie*. Königstein: Athenäum.

[228]

WINKEL, HARALD (1985), 'Der Glaube an die Beherrschbarkeit von Wirtschaftskrisen (1933–1970): Lehren aus der Weltwirtschaftskrise', in Gerhard Schulz (ed.), *Die Große Krise der dreißiger Jahre: Vom Niedergang der Weltwirtschaft zum Zweiten Weltkrieg*. Göttingen: Vandenhoeck & Ruprecht, 17–43.

WOLTER, ACHIM, and HASSE, ROLF H. (1997), 'Gemeinsame Beschäftigungspolitik: überfällig oder überflüssig?', *Wirtschaftsdienst*, 77: 386–9.

ZÜRN, MICHAEL (1995), 'The Challenge of Globalization and Individualization: A View from Europe', in Hans-Henrik Holm and Georg Sörensen (eds.), *Whose World Order? Uneven Globalization and the End of the Cold War*. Boulder, Colo.: Westview, 137–63.

——(1996), 'Über den Staat und die Demokratie im europäischen Mehrebenensystem', *Politische Vierteljahresschrift*, 37: 27–55.

INDEX